CVMBoK

A Guide to Customer Value Management

TELECOMS EDITION

Egidijus Pilypas

Šarūnas Chomentauskas

Silvia Gomez Dominguez

Kristine Raumane

Rokas Narkus

Exacaster

Published by Exacaster UAB,
J. Basanaviciaus 26, Vilnius LT-03224 Lithuania,
cvmbok@exacaster.com

While this publication is designed to provide accurate and authoritative information in regard to the subject matter covered, it is sold with the understanding that the publisher is not engaged in rendering legal, accounting, or other professional services. If legal advice or other expert assistance is required, the services of a competent professional person should be sought.
— *From the Declaration of Principles jointly adopted by a Committee of the American Bar Association and a Committee of Publishers and Associations*

Library of Congress Control Number:
Paperback ISBN: 978-609-96469-0-9
E-book ISBN: 978-609-96469-1-6

Contents

List of Figures

List of Acronyms

AI: Artificial intelligence

ARPU: Average revenue per user

BI: Business intelligence

CLV: Customer lifetime value

CVM: Customer value management

CX: Customer experience

DA: Data analytics

ETL: Extract, transform, load

FTTH: Fiber to the Home

GM: General management

IVR: Interactive voice response

KPI: Key performance indicator

ML: Machine learning

MLOps: Machine learning operations

NBA: Next best action

NBO: Next best offer

NPS: Net promoter score

PM: Product management

Pre2Post: Prepaid-to-postpaid

USSD: Unstructured supplementary service data

VAS: Value-added services

1. Embracing the Power of Customer Value Management

1.1 The Era of Customer Value Management

Telecoms today face a new reality: the era of growth through rapid customer acquisition has ended as markets have matured globally. Now, sustainable growth hinges on retaining and maximizing the value of the existing customer base through effective customer value management (CVM). While competitors can quickly replicate products, pricing, and offers, they cannot copy the unique way you treat your customers, the value you create for them, and how you retain their loyalty. This is where CVM becomes critical.

Consider the experience of Alberto Arimana Celis, Head of B2B CVM at Entel Peru:

"In 2019, when I began leading CVM in B2B at Entel Peru, our mobile churn rate was extremely high. I implemented significant changes—I restructured the organization, adjusted management focus, altered our approach with channels, and initiated weekly alignment meetings. We took ownership of customer communication; previously, no one did, and anyone could tell customers whatever they wanted. Through these efforts, over approximately two years, we reduced churn by 50 percent. It was an amazing achievement, and I'm proud of the huge work my team and I accomplished."

Telecoms are uniquely positioned to capitalize on CVM due to their mainly subscription-based business model, which offers distinct advantages:

- **Continuously used product:** Telecom services are used regularly and continuously. Unlike businesses that rely on one-time purchases, telecoms don't need to constantly find new customers to survive. For example, an appliance manufacturer sells a washing machine, and the customer might not make another purchase for years. In contrast, telecom customers use voice, data, and messaging services daily. This continuous usage allows telecoms to focus on ensuring that existing customers renew their subscriptions or keep paying for prepaid service, enhancing the value with each renewal.

- **Continuous relationship:** Telecoms maintain ongoing relationships with customers, often spanning over a decade, with regular communication cycles. In contrast, a furniture retailer may only interact with a customer during the purchase and delivery of items. After that, the relationship largely ends unless the customer initiates another purchase. Telecoms, however, engage with customers through monthly billing, service updates, and support interactions, fostering deeper engagement and loyalty.

- **Capability to analyze individual behaviors and needs:** Subscription customers provide a wealth of data that can be individually analyzed. Telecoms can track usage patterns, preferences, and service needs at a granular level. Many businesses lack access to such detailed customer information. For example, a beverage company like Coca-Cola cannot determine how many individual servings a specific customer consumed last month or identify their most valuable consumers. Their products are sold through intermediaries, and direct consumption data is not accessible.

- **Ownership of direct communication with customers:** Telecoms have direct communication channels with their customers—through call centers, telemarketing, digital platforms like email and apps, and in-person interactions at retail stores. This direct connection is a significant advantage. Many companies do not have this level of access. For example, car manufacturers often rely on dealerships for sales and customer interactions. They may not communicate directly with car owners unless there's a recall or service notification, limiting their ability to build relationships and offer personalized value.

These unique attributes create massive opportunities for growth through effective CVM. However, despite its potential, CVM is a relatively new and unstructured discipline. It is not taught in universities, and the number of CVM professionals is limited—approximately 3,000 to 4,000 globally—given that there are around 1,100 telecoms worldwide with an average of three CVM professionals in each. Furthermore, CVM is commercially sensitive—professionals in the same country rarely share their knowledge, making it one of the best-kept secrets in marketing.

Our mission is to change this paradigm. We aim to help organizations grow by employing state-of-the-art CVM practices. We are committed to making CVM professionals famous and elevating the discipline to its rightful place in the strategic growth of telecoms.

1.2 Customer Value Management Body of Knowledge (CVMBoK)

As every CVM professional knows, there are no comprehensive resources to guide them in mastering this complex field. This Customer Value Management Body of Knowledge (CVMBoK) aims to fill the gap, serving as the definitive guide to navigating the intricacies of CVM in the telecom sector.

The *CVMBoK* is designed to empower you to:

- **Strategically align your organization for CVM success:** Learn how to position CVM within your organization to maximize its impact on customer retention and average revenue per user (ARPU) growth.

- **Develop effective CVM programs:** Gain insights into the full CVM programs portfolio that drives the impact in your organization and are aligned with customer needs.

- **Build a robust CVM technology stack:** Understand the technological infrastructure needed to support CVM operations, from customer data platforms to real-time decisioning systems.

- **Foster cross-functional collaboration:** Discover strategies to break down silos and collaborate effectively with departments like Marketing, Sales, IT, and Customer Service.

By delving into the *CVMBoK*, you'll access actionable insights and best practices that address common challenges, such as siloed information, lack of standardized methodologies, and limited avenues for professional development. This unified framework is crafted by industry experts with decades of experience managing prepaid, postpaid, home services, and B2B customers.

Consider these reflections of fellow CVM practitioners:

> *"Unfortunately, we don't learn CVM at school. In the DRC [Democratic Republic of the Congo], there are no courses dedicated to CVM. You enter the industry and start working with data, trying to understand it and just sending out some offers. The recommended podcast is CVM Stories."*

— Thierry Awetimbi, CVM Manager at Vodacom Congo (no longer with the company)

> *"CVM is quite tough at the beginning because many practitioners don't have a single source of information. You learn from data science, but there was no comprehensive book on CVM until Exacaster launched the CVMBoK digital version and started sharing insights in the CVM Stories podcast. Before this, my information came from reading data science books and trying to imagine how to implement it in our organization."*

— Tommy Wahyudi, VP - Head of CVM Data Growth Strategy at Indosat Ooredoo

Our mission with the *CVMBoK* is clear: to elevate the discipline of CVM and support professionals like you in making a significant impact within your organizations. We aim to demystify CVM, provide the tools and knowledge necessary for success, and ultimately make CVM professionals renowned for their contributions to the telecom industry's growth.

1.3 Building the CVMBoK Through Global Collaboration

The *CVMBoK* is more than a guide—it's a collective achievement shaped by the experiences of CVM professionals from around the world. Recognizing that our industry's strength lies in shared wisdom, we've brought together insights from dozens of CVM professionals across all continents. They have contributed through podcasts, interviews, benchmark surveys, and direct feedback, enriching this resource with diverse perspectives.

These contributions come from professionals managing prepaid, postpaid, home services, and B2B customers in various markets. Participation in initiatives like the *CVM Stories* podcast has allowed customer value managers to discuss challenges and best practices openly. Through these candid conversations, we've gathered real-world examples that illustrate both the obstacles and successes in CVM implementation. Many of the quotes that you'll find in the guide are taken from these conversations.

The *CVM Benchmark* Survey has been another source of information, with many customer value managers sharing data that highlight current trends and common pain points in the industry. This collective input has shaped both insights about the current state in the industry and also the most popular strategies and frameworks presented in the *CVMBoK*.

This collaborative effort underscores the global nature of CVM and the universal challenges we face. By pooling our knowledge, we've created a resource that transcends geographical boundaries and offers practical solutions applicable worldwide.

We invite you to join this ongoing journey. Your experiences and insights are invaluable in keeping the *CVMBoK* dynamic and relevant. Together, we can continue to elevate the CVM profession and drive success across the telecom industry. For more information on getting involved also check out Chapter 6.

1.4 How to Use This Guide

CVMBoK is a comprehensive guide tailored for CVM professionals in the telecom industry. Whether you're a manager, a CVM practitioner, or part of a cross-functional team, this guide is designed to meet your needs and help you excel.

1.4.1 For Managers and Leaders

As a manager, focus on Chapters 2, 4, and 5 to align CVM with your organizational goals and understand the technical and organizational capabilities required for success. Chapter 2 explains the shift from product-centric to customer-centric approaches, highlights CVM's position within the organization, outlines key performance indicators (KPIs) essential for decision-making, and gives guidance on hiring the right talent. Chapter 4 gives insights on what technology investments might be necessary in your organization. Chapter 5 offers strategies for fostering effective collaboration across departments, ensuring that you CVM team has the necessary mandate and resources.

1.4.2 For Customer Value Management Practitioners

If you're a CVM practitioner, delve into Chapters 3, 4, and 5 to grasp the full scope of CVM. Chapter 3 provides actionable strategies for acquiring, growing, and retaining customers, covering topics like onboarding, upselling, loyalty programs, and churn management. Chapter 4 helps you navigate the complex technology landscape, understand architectural principles for a future-proof CVM tech stack, and master essential components like customer data platforms and real-time decisioning systems. Chapter 5 offers insights on how to collaborate with other departments effectively.

1.4.3 For Cross-functional Teams

For those in cross-functional teams, explore Chapter 5 to learn how collaboration with the CVM team can enhance overall performance. Understanding how CVM teams interact with your department allows you to contribute effectively to shared goals. By aligning your efforts with CVM initiatives, you can enhance customer engagement and drive organizational success.

2. The Role of Customer Value Management

CVM is a part of the broader discipline called marketing. Traditional marketing is grounded in Philip Kotler's renowned 4Ps framework—product, price, place, and promotion. The 4Ps have long guided businesses in creating offerings, setting prices, distributing products, and stimulating demand (see Figure 2.1).

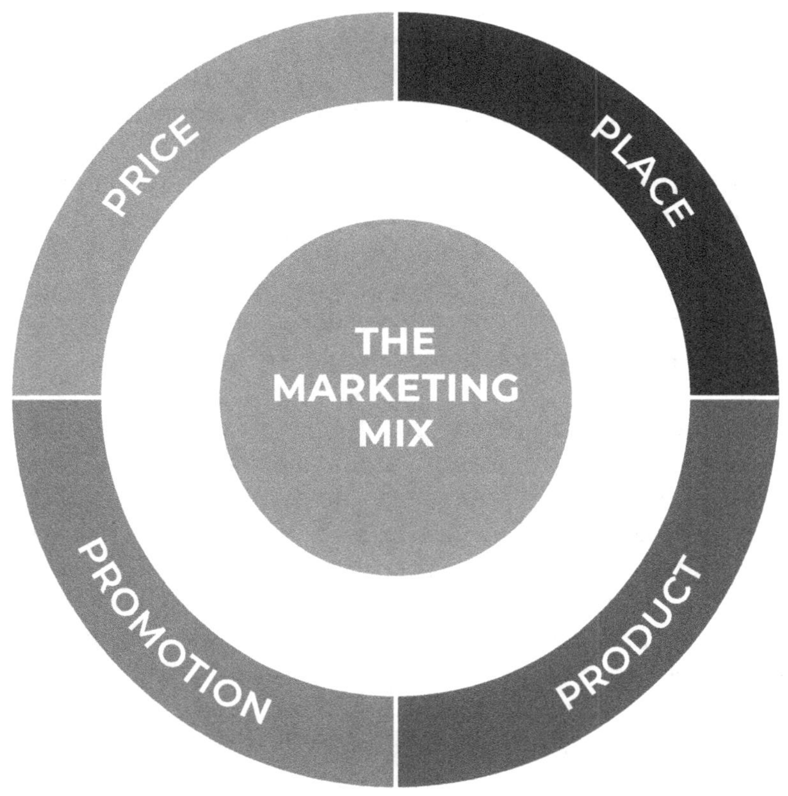

Figure 2.1: The 4Ps of Marketing

While this framework provides a solid foundation, it overlooks a crucial element: the customer.

2.1 The Transformation from a Product-centric to a Customer-centric Approach

In the beginning of the book we identified that telecoms are uniquely positioned to capitalize on CVM due to their subscription-based business model. Telecoms have:

- Continuous product usage
- Continuous relationships with customers
- The capability to analyze an individual customer's behaviors and needs
- Ownership of direct communication with customers

Traditional marketing focuses heavily on the 4Ps, emphasizing product features, competitive pricing, distribution channels, and promotional tactics to drive sales. And while effective in generating acquisition, this approach overlooks the unique characteristics of subscription-like products. Organizations that rely on the 4Ps are very product centric—they do not take into account the individual needs and experiences of customers, treating them as mere recipients rather than active participants in the value creation process.

CVM expands the 4P framework by integrating a customer-centric perspective. It balances the focus on products with a deep understanding of customer behaviors, preferences, and their value. For example, instead of promoting the same data plan for everyone, a CVM-driven approach might tailor the offer to specific customer segments by analyzing their actual usage patterns. A heavy data user will receive an offer for unlimited data with added value services, while casual users might be presented with a cost-effective plan with capped data options.

The beauty of CVM is that customer segmentation is limitless, and the ultimate goal is to deliver a true one-to-one communication experience. To achieve this goal, you should not just take a product perspective but also focus deeply on customer needs.

Embracing a customer-centric focus doesn't mean sidelining focus on business results. Instead, it signifies a shift from a transactional mindset that's focused on short-term gains (increased one-time sales), to a strategy that seeks greater business impact through long-term relationship-building. This approach emphasizes customer trust, loyalty, and customer advocacy, ultimately leading to sustained profitability.

2.1.1 Embracing Customer Value Principles

To make a customer-centric vision a reality, the CVM team must align the organization with fundamental customer value principles. These principles guide every action and shape how you interact with your customers, especially in customer-facing and product development roles. While each organization may have unique principles based on its strategy and brand promise, two stand out for their importance.

2.1.1.1 Principle #1: Always Act in the Customer's Best Interest

The foremost principle is to always act in the customer's best interest. This means prioritizing the customer's needs in every interaction. By doing so, you build trust and foster long-term relationships that enhance customer lifetime value (CLV). This principle permeates all aspects of your dealings with customers. For example, you avoid hidden fees and provide clear, straightforward contract terms. You simplify billing statements to make information easy to understand. You tailor offers to meet individual customer needs based on their usage patterns and preferences. You also anticipate customer needs and address potential issues before they escalate.

2.1.1.2 Principle #2: Always Deliver Value

The second critical principle is to consistently deliver value. You ensure that your products and services meet or exceed customer expectations. Delivering value can take many forms. Sometimes it means helping customers relocate their broadband service smoothly and without excessive charges. Other times it involves assisting customers in adopting new technologies like teaching them how to use the latest smartphone features. It could also be advising customers to upgrade to a larger plan to avoid the higher costs of add-ons and consumption fees even though they might be more profitable in the short term for the company.

By embracing these customer value principles, you move beyond a transactional mindset focused on short-term gains. Instead, you adopt a strategic approach that values long-term relationships, leading to sustained profitability and a stronger position in the market.

2.1.2 Five Customer Value Management Transformations

Implementing CVM brings profound changes to how telecoms operate. This shift towards customer centricity leads to five key transformations that reshape the organization.

1. **From a service-based to a whole-of-customer perspective:** Traditionally, telecoms analyze services like broadband, mobile plans, or digital offerings in isolation. This siloed perspective ignores how these services are used together and collectively shape the customer's experience. Adopting a holistic view means understanding the entire customer journey, considering all touchpoints, behaviors, and preferences. For example, a customer using both mobile and home internet services may value unified billing and seamless connectivity. By recognizing this, telecoms can offer integrated solutions that enhance satisfaction and strengthen loyalty across multiple services.

2. **From revenue-based decisions to value and profitability-based decisions:** In a product-centric approach, decisions prioritize immediate revenue and conversions for specific products or offers. This approach can lead to multiple uncoordinated messages targeting the same customer, diminishing the customer experience (CX) and increasing churn over time. Shifting to a customer-centric approach involves basing decisions on customer value and profitability metrics like CLV and margin. By aligning products and services with customer needs, telecoms can foster sustainable, long-term relationships. For example, offering personalized plan upgrades based on a customer's usage patterns can increase CLV while reducing churn.

3. **From mass marketing campaigns to personalized, targeted marketing campaigns:** Historically, telecoms deployed large-scale mass marketing campaigns aimed at reaching as many customers as possible. While such campaigns had broad reach, they were often expensive and resulted in generic messages with low engagement rates. The move towards a customer-centric approach involves shifting to highly targeted and personal-

ized marketing campaigns, powered by artificial intelligence (AI) and advanced analytics. These campaigns are designed to deliver the right message through the most effective channel, whether that be SMS, email, in-store or on social media. This approach ensures higher conversion rates and stronger engagement, reducing the cost of customer acquisition and improving overall campaign effectiveness.

4. **From siloed to cross-functional and collaborative teams:** A customer-centric approach necessitates breaking down organizational silos to foster cross-functional teamwork. Collaboration between marketing, operations, customer service, and IT ensures that every team aligns with a shared customer-first strategy. For example, when launching a new service, coordinated efforts across departments can provide a seamless CX—from initial marketing to service activation and ongoing support. This collaborative approach enables faster decision-making and more agile responses to customer needs.

5. **From individual team goals to organization-wide strategic KPIs:** To become truly customer-centric, CVM helps to shift the organization's focus from isolated performance metrics to strategic KPIs that inspire the entire organization. These shared KPIs—such as net promoter score (NPS), churn reduction, and customer satisfaction—ensure that every team understands their role in delivering value to the customer and achieving the organization's goals. Aligning the teams towards shared objectives drives both accountability and collective success.

2.1.3 Transformation Enablers

Technology and data play a critical role in operationalizing these transformations. Modern CVM relies on integrating data, AI, and customer intelligence into campaign automation platforms. By harnessing vast datasets—from call records to social media activity—and applying machine learning (ML) models, telecoms have shifted from manual campaigns to real-time, personalized customer engagement.
Automation engines enable dynamic interactions tailored to individual preferences and behaviors. For example, rules and predictive algorithms can trigger personalized offers based on a customer's data

usage or billing history, ensuring that each communication is relevant and timely.

CVM decisions are guided by four key types of advanced analytics:

- **Descriptive analytics:** Understanding past behaviors, such as service usage trends

- **Predictive analytics:** Forecasting future actions, like identifying customers likely to churn

- **Preventive analytics:** Anticipating risks to enable proactive interventions

- **Prescriptive analytics:** Recommending optimal actions based on predictive insights

These analytics, powered by AI and enriched with thousands of customer attributes, feed next best action (NBA) frameworks to identify the most optimal action to take with a customer at any given time. By delivering the right message at the right time through the appropriate channel, telecoms enhance CXs and build stronger relationships.

The impact of robust CVM strategies is profound. Telecom providers that embrace CVM report higher customer retention rates, increased CLV, and improved NPS. End-to-end automation enhances operational efficiency by streamlining processes and enabling swift, accurate responses to customer needs.

Moreover, CVM frameworks equip telecoms to respond proactively to market challenges. During service disruptions, for example, CVM systems can initiate personalized communications to affected customers, mitigating churn and preserving brand reputation. Continual learning from customer interactions ensures that engagement strategies evolve, delivering consistent results and sustaining a competitive edge.

In essence, CVM transforms telecoms by bridging the gap between traditional product-centric approaches and the modern demand for customer-centric experiences. By placing the customer at the heart of every decision and leveraging technology to personalize interactions, telecoms can navigate the industry's complexities and thrive in an era defined by change.

2.2 The Customer Value Management Role Within the Organization

CVM's transformative impact stems from its cross-functional nature. It touches every department—from Marketing and Sales to Product Development and IT, all the way to Customer Service and Finance. However, for CVM to orchestrate such widespread organizational changes, it must be positioned strategically within the organization's hierarchy.

Based on the *CVM Trends 2025* report, 90 percent of CVM teams are within the Marketing or Commercial departments where eventually they report to one of the following:

- **Chief Commercial Officer (CCO):** When housed under the CCO, the CVM team intersects with marketing, sales, product development, and customer service. This setup enables the CVM team to infuse customer value insights across diverse commercial activities, ensuring that customer value is at the heart of all commercial decisions.

- **Chief Marketing Officer (CMO):** When viewed as a marketing function, the CVM team reports to the CMO, aligning with marketing communication strategies and initiatives.

- **Chief Customer Officer (CCO):** In some organizations, marketing and customer functions are merged under a CCO, who integrates marketing, sales, and customer-service.

- **CEO or Board of Directors:** In organizations prioritizing customer-centricity, CVM may report directly to the CEO or have board-level representation, underscoring its critical role in shaping the organization's strategic direction.

To drive transformations effectively, the CVM team must receive robust support from C-level executives and hold a clear mandate to influence changes across all functions. However, based on the same *CVM Trends* report you can see that half of CVM teams report to the heads of departments instead of reporting directly to the C-suite. This means that most CVM teams are still treated as mainly operational roles without a major strategic impact on the organization's growth (see Figure 2.2).

To what level of seniority does the CVM function report within your organization?

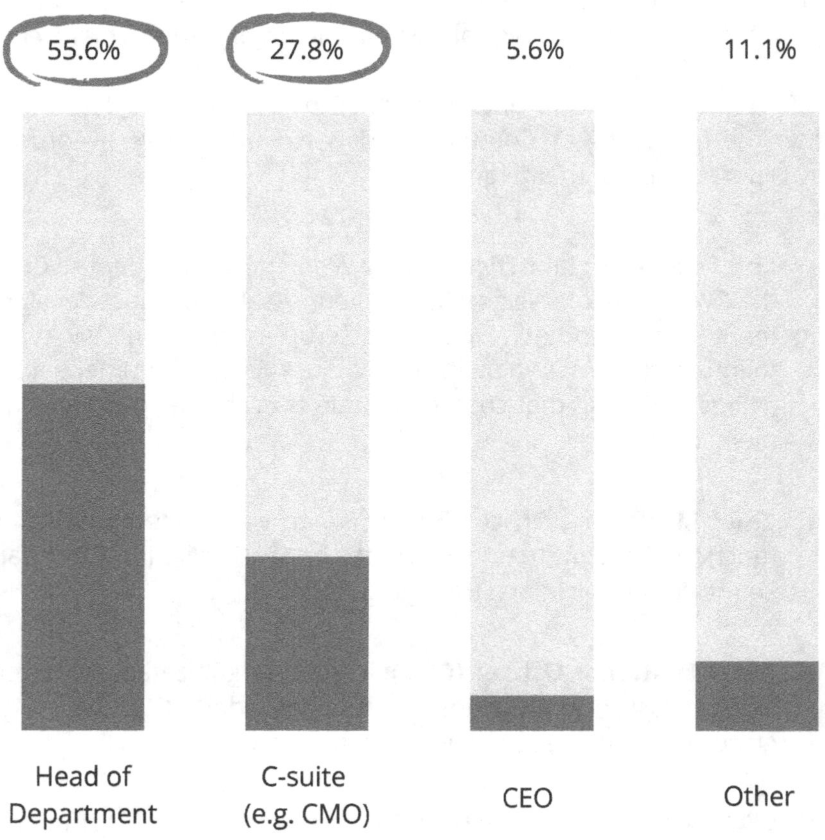

Figure 2.2: Level of Seniority that CVM Professionals Report To

Silvia Gomez Dominguez, Senior Director, Customer Solutions, underscores the importance of this high-level positioning:

"In my experience, CVM roles have always reported into the C-Level. It is crucial that CVM is seated at the right level because it requires influencing almost every single department in the business. They can report either to a CMO or a Chief Commercial Officer, reflecting the marketing-commercial mix that is most common."

Without strong C-level sponsorship, CVM teams may struggle to enact the changes necessary for true customer-centric transformation. Marek Wiktor Grabowski, B2C Customer Value Management Director at Orange Poland, highlights this challenge:

"There is a need for C-Level sponsorship, sometimes even CEO sponsorship. Different stakeholders in the organization hold significant power, so it is important to have a good sponsor. A marketing director heavily involved with data and adept at articulating CVM's impact can help, but C-level support is indispensable."

CVM often introduces initiatives that challenge established practices, which can meet resistance without executive backing. For example, implementing an AI-driven NBA framework might require significant investment and cross-departmental cooperation. Such a strategic move demands endorsement from top leadership to allocate resources and prioritize the project.

Furthermore, educating C-level executives about the strategic value of CVM is essential. Tommy Wahyudi, VP - Head of CVM Data Growth Strategy at Indosat Ooredoo, shares his insights:

"Not so many C-level executives understand how CVM works. They see CVM as just upselling or maybe selling cheap, giving discounts to the customer. That's what a lot of CVM practitioners get addressed with— you're just selling cheap products to your customer, and that's why you are growing. Well that is not the case. We trade off the yield with the subscriber to make them spend more. Eventually, after experiments that prove revenue increases, the C-level gets educated. It's a long journey because it takes time for people to understand how CVM works."

2.3 Customer Value Management Key Performance Indicators (KPIs)

Customer value management plays a pivotal commercial role in telecoms, aiming to drive significant business impact. To measure this impact effectively, focus on three primary categories of KPIs, with an optional fourth related to operational efficiency:

1. **Revenue and profitability:** Metrics such as total revenue from the customer base, ARPU, and profitability per customer (not product or service) provide immediate insights into the financial health of the organization.

2. **Customer base size and retention:** Indicators like customer base size, churn rates, and product onboarding rates highlight the stability and growth potential of your customer base as well as product penetration within the customer base.

3. **CX:** Metrics such as net NPS and customer satisfaction score (CSAT) assess the quality of customer interactions and the likelihood of customers recommending your services.

4. **Operational efficiency:** Metrics related to the agility and effectiveness of internal processes, such as the time and effort required to launch and maintain all of your campaigns, offers, and the associated salary, technology, and many other categories of costs.

Balancing these KPIs is crucial for sustainable growth. While revenue and profitability show immediate financial performance, focusing solely on them can be shortsighted. Without considering customer retention and experience, gains in revenue may be undermined by high churn rates later. For example, aggressively promoting upsells without regard for customer satisfaction might boost short-term revenue but lead to long-term customer loss.

Customer retention metrics emphasize the importance of keeping existing customers engaged and satisfied. Retaining customers is often more cost-effective than acquiring new ones. A telecom monitoring churn rates closely can implement targeted retention campaigns, such as offering personalized discounts or proactively fixing the issues that cause customers to leave.

CX metrics like NPS and CSAT provide insights into how customers perceive your services. A high NPS indicates strong customer advocacy, which can lead to organic growth through referrals. For example, improving network reliability might increase customer satisfaction scores, leading to higher retention rates.

Operational efficiency metrics, though sometimes overlooked, are critical for enhancing your responsiveness to market changes and customer needs. Think of it as how much time the CVM team spends on strategic growth opportunities versus the time they spend on operational issues. Streamlining the time it takes to develop and launch new campaigns gives the organization a competitive edge. By automating campaign management processes, you can reduce time-to-market and swiftly respond to competitor moves.

Using CLV as a unifying metric helps integrate revenue, retention, and CX areas. CLV estimates the total net profit expected from a customer over their entire relationship with you. By focusing on CLV, you align short-term financial goals with long-term customer loyalty and satisfaction.

As Marek Wiktor Grabowski, B2C Customer Value Management Director at Orange Poland, emphasizes:

> *"The ultimate KPI is the revenue from the customer base, comprising existing customer purchases, new purchases, and increased value by adding additional services. You need to work on the entire base; that is the scope of CVM."*

Measuring the effects of your CVM initiatives is essential for success. Marek adds:

> *"We have introduced a universal control group of customers not touched proactively. We compare CVM results versus that group. Control groups per specific campaigns are also useful to gain insights."*

Silvia Gomez Dominguez, Senior Director, Customer Solutions, highlights the importance of aligning KPIs across the organization:

> *"It is important that each part of the business has specific KPIs, but overall, we are all trying to be customer-centric. That way, we'll be able to achieve customer metrics like NPS, financial metrics like lifetime value, CapEx targets, ROI—all of those."*

Elchin Gulmammadov, Group Marketing Director at Azerconnect Group, stresses the need to focus on key inputs:

> *"We are tracking our active customers daily. This is one of the key KPIs for our CVM team because these customers bring revenue. Revenue is the result; we keep our eyes closely on the key inputs because revenue is the output."*

He also advocates for keeping the number of KPIs manageable:

> *"I believe in keeping a minimum number of KPIs so that everyone can focus and improve on those. For my team, we keep a maximum of three KPIs per team or division."*

In practice, CVM professionals must navigate the interplay among these metrics to drive sustainable growth. Overemphasizing revenue might erode customer satisfaction, leading to higher churn. Conversely, focusing solely on CX without regard to profitability may not be sustainable either.

By using CLV as the guiding metric, you can balance these priorities effectively. This approach ensures that your strategies not only drive immediate financial results but also build long-term customer relationships, leading to sustained profitability and a stronger position in the telecom industry.

2.4 The Evolving Identity of Customer Value Management Roles

The CVM role is multifaceted and often carries various titles. Common titles include Customer Value Manager, Customer Base Manager, Customer Relationship Manager, and Customer Retention Manager. Other variations include Customer Lifecycle Manager, Customer Engagement Manager, High-Value Customers Manager, Prepaid/Postpaid Manager, Mass Segment Manager, Consumer Products and Services Manager, and Product Marketing Manager. This diversity reflects the cross-functional nature of CVM but leads to a lack of standardization.

The emergence of these different titles has happened organically. As CVM responsibilities differ across organizations, so do the job titles. Each title highlights specific facets of the role, emphasizing the wide range of functions that CVM covers. However, this inconsistency can cause confusion within the industry. For example, a CVM manager in one telecom might focus just on customer retention, while in another they might handle customer segmentation, pricing, and targeted marketing campaigns.

Recognizing this issue, one of the objectives of this *Customer Value Management Body of Knowledge (CVMBoK)* is to establish industry-wide standards. By creating a common framework, we aim to unify the understanding of CVM roles and responsibilities. And although it's essential to acknowledge that organizations approach CVM differently, adopting standardized titles can enhance clarity.

Using the words "Customer Value" or "Customer Value Management" in the title as a standard practice is a practical solution. Titles could range from "VP Customer Value Management" to "Customer Value Management Director, Leader, Specialist," depending on hierarchy and seniority. This approach not only clarifies the role's identity but also underscores the strategic importance of CVM within the organization. For example, a telecom that adopts the title Customer Value Analyst signals a focus on analyzing customer data to drive value, making the role's purpose clear to both internal teams and external partners.

Standardizing titles is more than mere semantics; it fosters a shared language that enhances collaboration and knowledge sharing across the telecom industry. As we work towards establishing these standards, we acknowledge the evolving identity of CVM roles. Bringing clarity and cohesion to this critical function is essential for achieving our mission of making CVM professionals famous.

2.5 Selecting the Right Talent: The Key to Customer Value Management Success

According to the *CVM Trends 2025* report, about 50 percent of CVM teams cannot demonstrate a meaningful contribution to their organization's revenue growth (see Figure 2.3). This concerning statistic prompts a closer examination of the underlying causes.

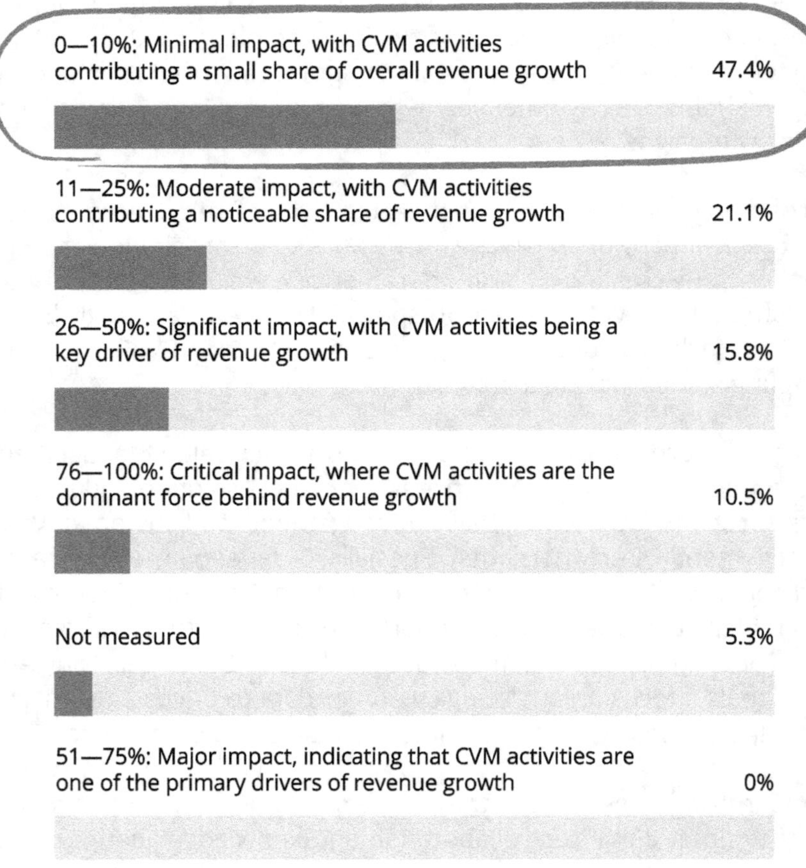

Figure 2.3: CVM's Contribution to an Organization's Revenue Growth

CVM teams often point to technical issues that limit their success: poor data quality, lack of a unified customer view, limited omnichannel capabilities, and long development times for new ML models or offers. While these challenges are genuine, they are often not the primary reason for limited impact. The core issue usually lies elsewhere.

The true determinant of CVM success is hiring the right professionals and providing them with the necessary mandates and C-level support. Because the CVM role is exceptionally dynamic and complex, it
requires a unique blend of skills to navigate its multifaceted nature
effectively.

2.5.1 Skills Needed to Be a Successful Customer Value Management Professional

Based on *CVM Trends 2025* research, 75 percent of CVM professionals spend at least half of their time on ad-hoc tasks due to the highly
dynamic environment (see Figure 2.4). For example, they might need
to react quickly when a competitor launches a new data plan, adjust
strategies when introducing a new service, fix a failed campaign's communication, or address sudden increases in churn. These unexpected
challenges demand immediate attention and agile responses.

**How much time is spent on strategic initiatives (planner and
part of broader vision) vs. ad hoc activity (reactive, tactical
activity)?**

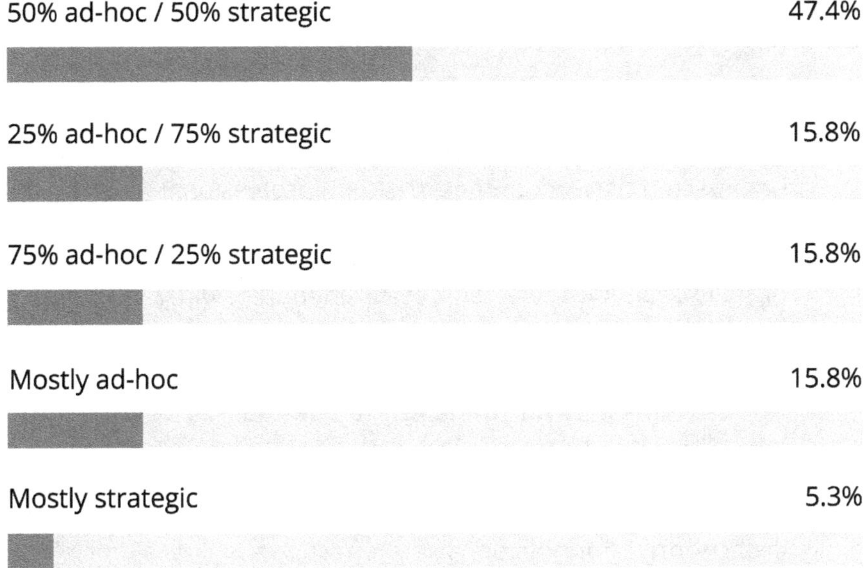

Figure 2.4: Time Spent on Strategic Initiatives vs. Ad-hoc Activities

In addition, CVM teams must collaborate with over twenty different functions within the organization. They need to be technically savvy to create effective campaigns, discuss technical integrations, and stay updated on the latest digital trends. Strong analytical skills are essential for conducting raw data analysis and generating insightful reports. Figure 2.5 shows where typical CVM teams spend most of their time.

Given these complexities, selecting the right talent for CVM roles is crucial. While specific requirements may vary, several key qualities consistently enable professionals to excel in CVM.

- **Broad professional experience:** CVM professionals need to think strategically while managing operational details. Balancing long-term objectives with immediate tasks ensures that daily actions contribute to overarching goals. Seasoned professionals bring valuable knowledge and insights that help navigate these complexities. Their experience allows them to anticipate challenges and devise effective strategies. Amit Khanna, Marketing Consultant at MTN Ivory Coast, explains this:

  "As a marketing manager, you need to wear different hats. At times, you need to think as a marketer, a technical expert, and an analytical expert. At the end of the day, everybody's mission is to improve the overall business."

- **Flexibility and agility:** Every day in CVM brings new challenges, many beyond one's control. For example, if a telecom faces an unexpected network outage, the CVM professional must quickly adjust customer communications to manage expectations. This role will be by design extremely dynamic. For this reason, CVM professionals must be capable of adapting swiftly to changing business contexts and needs.

- **An entrepreneurial mindset:** Successful CVM professionals think like startup CEOs of their domain. They focus on business impact, prioritizing customer needs, and overcoming obstacles to achieve results. This entrepreneurial approach drives innovation and effectiveness. As Amit Khanna, Marketing Consultant at MTN Ivory Coast, emphasizes:

What other business activities fall under the CVM team's scope, and how much of the team's time is spent on them?

	Not relevant	<5%	5—10%	11—20%	21—30%	>31%
Customer data management	11.1%	22.2%	22.2%	0%	22.2%	22.2%
Consents management	33.3%	44.4%	5.6%	0%	5.6%	11.1%
Tech development roadmapping	38.9%	16.7%	27.8%	5.6%	5.6%	5.6%
Business requirements gathering	16.7%	16.7%	27.8%	5.6%	11.1%	22.2%
Marketing campaign management	5.6%	11.1%	27.8%	0%	0%	55.6%
Marketing channel execution (e.g. paid media)	27.8%	11.1%	22.2%	11.1%	5.6%	22.2%
Transactional communication (e.g. T&C updates, legal notices)	16.7%	16.7%	22.2%	16.7%	0%	27.8%
Customer segment creation	11.1%	11.1%	38.9%	5.6%	11.1%	22.2%
Building reports & dashboards	5.6%	11.1%	16.7%	22.2%	11.1%	33.3%
Raw data analysis (e.g. with SQL or Python)	27.8%	11.1%	5.6%	11.1%	11.1%	33.3%

Figure 2.5: Where CVM Teams Spend Their Time

- **High energy and strong project management skill:** CVMs are like conductors orchestrating a symphony. They must align and empower multiple functions within the organization to achieve their goals. This level of coordination requires substantial energy and capacity to achieve results not through authority but through influence. Without strong project management skills, CVM professionals will not be able to achieve the impact they need.

- **Technical and analytical savvy:** A strong grasp of technology and analytics is essential. CVM professionals must understand the nitty gritty of campaign automation, data analysis, and digital trends to make informed decisions and drive performance. As Silvia Gomez Dominguez, Senior Director, Customer Solutions, notes:

"Even being a senior leader, I like to stay close to the technology and the data. Understanding how things work helps me make better decisions day-to-day."

As Tommy Wahyudi, VP - Head of CVM Data Growth Strategy at Indosat Ooredoo, highlights:

"CVM is a mix between data science and marketing. Not many understand that in CVM, data science meets marketing—that's where all the game is played."

By hiring professionals who possess these qualities and providing them strong C-level support, telecoms can unlock the full potential of CVM. This approach ensures that CVM teams can navigate the dynamic landscape, collaborate effectively across functions, and drive significant business impact.

3. The Work of Customer Value Management Professionals

Acting in the customer's best interest and creating value can often feel like an overwhelming challenge, given the myriads of opportunities and the noise that comes with them. To navigate this complexity, CVM professionals need a structured approach that aligns their efforts with strategic goals and maximizes impact.

This chapter introduces the CVM Portfolio concept, which helps to identify CVM programs and initiatives based on three fundamental pillars—acquire, grow, and retain. Additionally, we introduce the CVM Canvas idea, which helps structure the main components of each initiative and serves as a blueprint for implementation.

3.1 The Customer Value Management Portfolio

The CVM Portfolio offers a high-level framework that enables CVM professionals to concentrate on activities that deliver maximum value (see Figure 3.1). To optimize their effectiveness, CVM professionals must distinguish between two categories of activities:

1. **CVM-driven impact:** Initiatives led and managed directly by the CVM function

2. **CVM-supported activities:** Organization initiatives led by other departments, where CVM contributes

Understanding this distinction is crucial. By focusing on CVM-driven impact, CVM professionals can allocate resources to areas where they have the most control and can directly influence outcomes. This focus ensures that efforts are not scattered, and that strategic objectives are met efficiently. Meanwhile, recognizing CVM-supported activities allows CVM professionals to collaborate effectively with other departments, contributing to their objectives without losing sight of their primary responsibilities.

CVM-driven impact centers around three fundamental pillars:

- **Acquire:** This is about adding new customers to your base by facilitating a seamless onboarding process for new customers or targeting former customers who have switched to competitors. For example, when a customer purchases a prepaid SIM card, CVM professionals can ensure that they receive immediate activation support, welcome messages, and guidance on initial top-ups. Programs under this pillar include customer onboarding, prepaid-to-postpaid (Pre2Post) migration, relocation support, referral programs, and win-back campaigns.

- **Grow:** This is about creating more value for your customers. A practical example is offering a postpaid customer an exclusive data bundle upgrade based on their increased data usage. Initiatives here encompass upsell and core services cross-sell campaigns, loyalty programs, and promoting value-added services (VAS) like international roaming packages or device insurance.

- **Retain:** This is about proactively preventing churn by addressing customer needs before issues escalate. For example, if data analytics indicate that a customer is experiencing frequent dropped calls, CVM professionals can reach out with solutions or compensatory offers. Programs include proactive retention strategies, cancellation management, involuntary churn prevention, and timely intervention with save offers when customers express a desire to cancel.

Simultaneously, CVM-supported activities involve collaborating with other departments on initiatives that affect the CX:

- **Legal and financial communications:** Work with finance teams to ensure that billing statements are clear and that payment reminders are customer-friendly. For example, you might simplify invoice layouts to reduce customer confusion and calls to customer service.

- **CX communications:** Partner with product management, marketing, and customer service teams to enhance product updates,

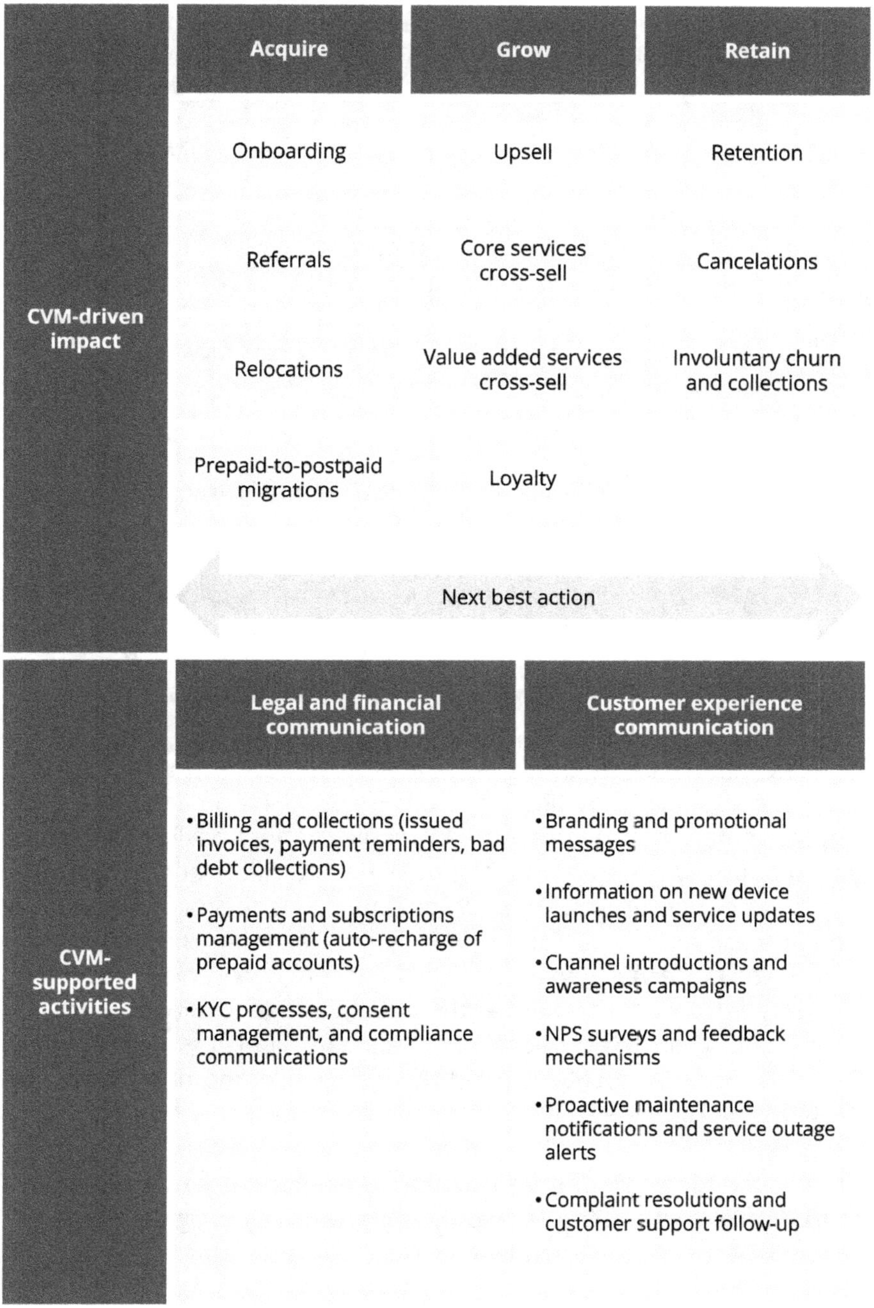

CVM-driven impact	Acquire	Grow	Retain
	Onboarding	Upsell	Retention
	Referrals	Core services cross-sell	Cancelations
	Relocations	Value added services cross-sell	Involuntary churn and collections
	Prepaid-to-postpaid migrations	Loyalty	

Next best action

CVM-supported activities	Legal and financial communication	Customer experience communication
	• Billing and collections (issued invoices, payment reminders, bad debt collections) • Payments and subscriptions management (auto-recharge of prepaid accounts) • KYC processes, consent management, and compliance communications	• Branding and promotional messages • Information on new device launches and service updates • Channel introductions and awareness campaigns • NPS surveys and feedback mechanisms • Proactive maintenance notifications and service outage alerts • Complaint resolutions and customer support follow-up

Figure 3.1: The CVM Portfolio

branding messages, and feedback mechanisms. An illustration is contributing to the development of an NPS survey that accurately captures customer sentiments and provides actionable insights.

By clearly separating CVM-driven and CVM-supported activities, CVM professionals can prioritize their efforts effectively. This distinction prevents resource dilution and ensures that CVM professionals have a significant impact on customer engagement, satisfaction, and loyalty. It allows them to lead initiatives where they can drive results while also providing valuable support to organization-wide projects without overextending their capacity.

According to Silvia Gomez Dominguez, Senior Director, Customer Solutions,

> *"A CVM Portfolio approach empowers CVM teams to channel their energy into impactful actions rather than getting caught up in complexity. The clarity provided by a structured approach drives effectiveness, customer satisfaction, and ultimately, business value."*

The importance of focusing the CVM team on the most impactful programs is supported by findings from the *CVM Trends 2025* research. Approximately half of telecom companies report having well-established onboarding, upselling, cross-selling, retention, and cancellation management programs. These areas reflect a strong focus on securing revenue early in the customer journey and retaining existing customers. However, fewer than a quarter of telecom companies report high maturity in more customer-centric initiatives like loyalty, relocations, or prepaid-to-postpaid migrations. This gap highlights opportunities for CVM professionals to expand their influence and drive long-term growth (See Figure 3.2).

In the upcoming sections, we'll explore these fundamental pillars—acquire, grow, and retain—in depth, along with key programs that can help telecoms and their leaders succeed.

What typical CVM programs does your team currently work on, and how mature are they?

	Fully mature	Developing	Early stages	No longer live	Not attempted	Not relevant
Onboarding	36.8%	31.6%	15.8%	5.3%	5.3%	5.3%
Price plans & offers campaigns	57.9%	31.6%	10.5%	0%	0%	0%
Up-sell	47.4%	31.6%	15.8%	0%	5.3%	0%
Cross-sell	42.1%	26.3%	21.1%	5.3%	5.3%	0%
Retention	42.1%	36.8%	15.8%	0%	0%	5.3%
Loyalty programme	10.5%	31.6%	26.3%	5.3%	15.8%	10.5%
Cancellation & winback	47.4%	15.8%	10.5%	10.5%	10.5%	5.3%
Device lifecycle management	26.3%	21.1%	15.8%	0%	26.3%	10.5%
Referrals programme	0%	21.1%	31.6%	10.5%	31.6%	5.3%
Roaming services management	21.1%	15.8%	21.1%	0%	15.8%	26.3%
Payments & billing experience management	31.6%	26.3%	15.8%	0%	15.8%	10.5%
Proactive customer service	21.1%	26.3%	15.8%	15.8%	15.8%	5.3%
Next best offer/ Next best action/ Next best experience (NBO/NBA/NBX)	26.3%	26.3%	21.1%	10.5%	5.3%	10.5%
Lifestage events (e.g. house movers)	11.1%	16.7%	27.8%	0%	22.2%	22.2%
Pre- to postpaid migration	9.1%	18.2%	18.2%	9.1%	9.1%	36.4%
Digital channels development	9.1%	45.5%	36.4%	0%	9.1%	0%

Figure 3.2: CVM Programs Maturity

3.2 The Customer Value Management Canvas

Turning the CVM Portfolio into real-world outcomes can be daunting. Telecom environments are complex, and initiatives usually involve multiple teams—each with its own responsibilities, priorities, and performance metrics. In such a setting, it is easy for even the best-planned programs to get lost in day-to-day operations. To counter this, CVM professionals need a unifying framework that sets clear objectives, defines responsibilities, and aligns stakeholders.

The CVM Canvas meets this need by providing a structured view of each CVM initiative. This tool ensures that every participant understands the initiative's purpose, how it will be executed, what resources are needed, and how success will be measured. Built on the PACE model—Purpose, Approach, Capabilities, and Evaluation—the CVM Canvas simplifies complex projects, prevents key details from slipping through the cracks, and keeps teams focused on delivering value (see Figure 3.3).

3.2.1 Purpose

Purpose explains why the initiative is being launched and how it supports broader corporate strategies. By articulating both the strategic alignment and the customer benefits, teams can work confidently, knowing their collective effort moves the organization in the right direction.
For instance, you may want to launch a postpaid cross-selling program to encourage existing customers to adopt home services, thus promoting product convergence. The Purpose section clarifies why convergence is a strategic priority—highlighting how it strengthens customer loyalty and increases ARPU—while also emphasizing the value for customers, such as enhanced service bundles, easier billing, and potential cost savings.

3.2.2 Approach

Approach describes how to reach the target audience, deliver tangible value, and guide the organization's efforts. By defining key elements like segmentation, offers, and channels, CVM professionals create a roadmap that multiple departments can follow consistently. Although details can grow complex during implementation, three main areas

The Customer Value Management Canvas:
Program Template

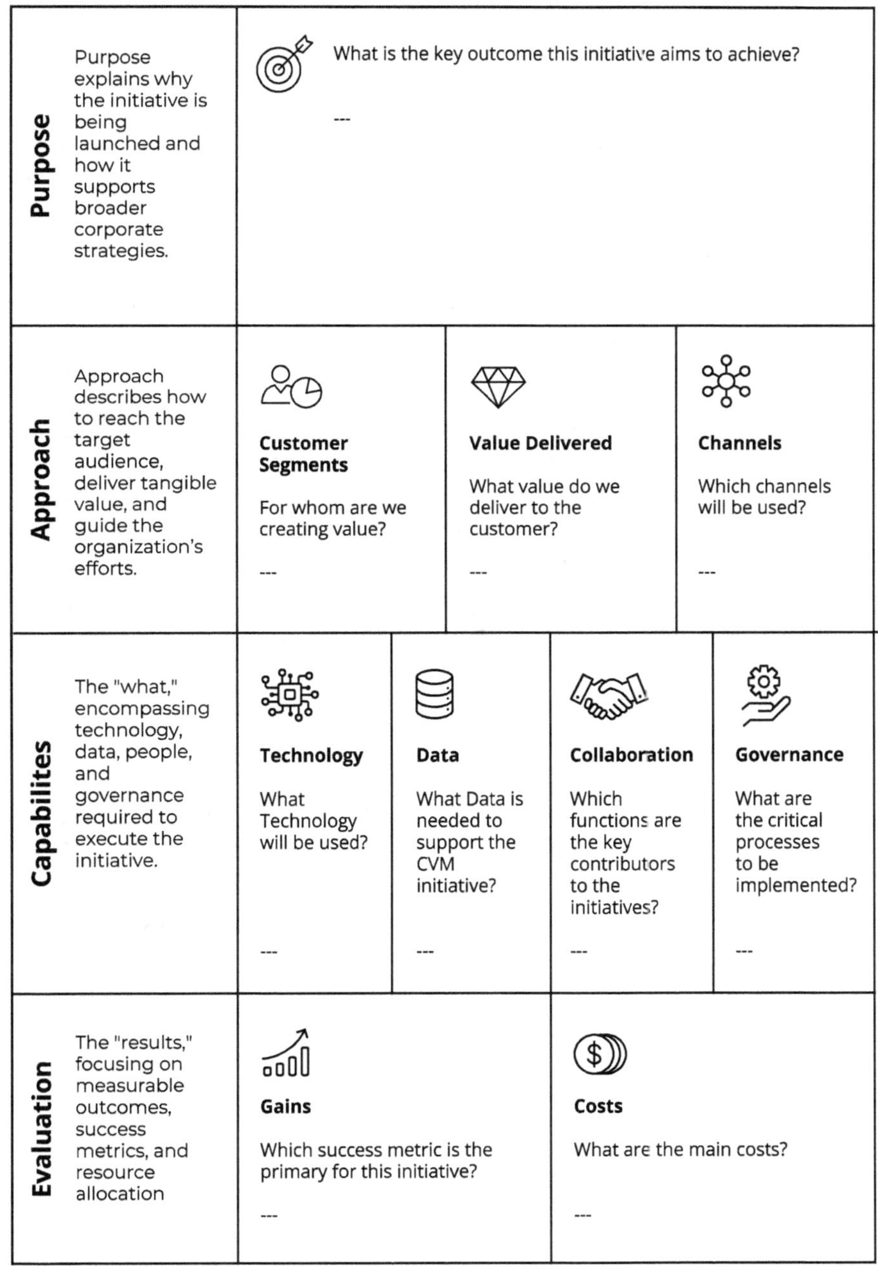

Figure 3.3: The CVM Canvas

must always be clear:

- **Customer segments:** Identify which audience groups will receive the offer or communication, specifying characteristics that differentiate each segment.

- **Value delivered:** Show what benefits or improvements customers gain by participating in the initiative, such as additional data allowances or bundled discounts.

- **Communication channels:** Outline how you will deliver these offers and messages.

Continuing the example of convergence, the Approach section could define distinct segments (e.g., postpaid customers with no fixed broadband service, or home internet customers without postpaid mobile). It would specify the added value for each segment (e.g., double data caps or faster broadband speeds for subscribers who move to a convergence plan) and list the primary communication channels for spreading the word (e.g., direct outbound calls, in-store communication, SMS, email, and in-app notifications.)

3.2.3 Capabilities

Capabilities cover the human, technical, and operational resources required to execute the initiative. Identifying these needs helps CVM teams gather the right experts, secure the right technologies, and create streamlined processes before launch. To organize these efforts, the CVM Canvas focuses on:

- **Technology:** Determine which platforms, software tools, and product features are essential for implementing the initiative.

- **Data:** Specify the data sources, analytical processes, and other key metrics you will rely on to deliver the initiative.

- **People:** Pinpoint the teams and roles that must collaborate to achieve the shared goals.

- **Governance:** Define the decision-making and reporting process-es that will keep everyone informed and accountable, such as regular cross-functional check-ins or monthly executive reviews.

In the convergence example, the Technology requirement might be a billing system upgrade that consolidates multiple services into a single invoice. Data needs might include identifying households with partial service usage. People considerations could involve a dedicated cross-functional task force—spanning IT, data analysts, and frontline sales—to ensure consistent execution. Governance might include a monthly steering committee to review performance metrics and re-solve issues.

3.2.4 Evaluation

Evaluation clarifies how you will measure success, monitor costs, and ensure that the initiative remains on track. By outlining expected gains and associated costs, you establish the basis for calculating ROI and making any necessary adjustments along the way. Key areas include:

- **Gains:** Specify the metrics that reflect the initiative's impact, such as higher ARPU, reduced churn, or improved customer sat-isfaction scores.

- **Costs:** Track the resources—financial and human—needed to deploy and maintain the initiative. This helps you validate fea-sibility and ensures that investment aligns with strategic goals.

In the case of a convergence program, you might measure gains by monitoring the share of customers who adopt combined mobile and broadband services, calculating the incremental revenue per user, and tracking churn reduction over time. Costs could include system up-grades, sales training, and marketing campaigns aimed at educating customers about the benefits of convergence.

As we continue, we will see how using the CVM Canvas brings clarity to all CVM programs. Armed with this framework, CVM professionals can better manage telecom's inherent complexity, stay focused on strate-gic goals, and adapt to emerging challenges in a competitive market-place.

3.3 Acquire

The first CVM Portfolio pillar is "acquire" and it groups initiatives related to new customers. Acquiring new customers goes beyond simply increasing subscriber numbers—it's about delivering a memorable first experience that builds the foundation for lasting relationships. The acquire pillar emphasizes initiatives designed to onboard and activate customers effectively, ensuring that they quickly recognize the value of your services and begin using them. Turning new customers into loyal, long-term advocates is the core objective of this pillar.

As the customer base grows, new opportunities arise, such as leveraging existing customers to drive acquisitions through referral programs, enhancing value by transitioning customers from prepaid to postpaid plans, supporting repurchases when life changes occur (e.g., relocation), and re-engaging lapsed customers. The programs in this pillar focus on growing the customer base in a strategic, sustainable, and impactful manner.

 **3.3.1 Onboarding**

3.3.1.1 Purpose

Onboarding ensures that customers begin using your services smoothly and fully. By delivering a clear and structured welcome experience, you establish trust, help customers adopt your services seamlessly, encourage timely payments, and reduce early churn. This sets the stage for a long-term, mutually beneficial relationship. When customers feel valued and supported from the outset, their satisfaction and loyalty naturally increase.

3.3.1.2 Approach

The onboarding program typically focuses on new customers during their initial phase—often the first 90 days after they purchase your service. In more advanced programs, you can shift to an objective-based model that tracks each customer's actual service adoption milestones rather than relying solely on time. The essence remains the same: ensure that customers quickly and easily start using all the services they purchased.

From the customer's perspective, the primary value of onboarding is a seamless and hassle-free experience. To deliver on this promise, your onboarding plan should address four key areas:

1. Welcome and activation
2. Product education
3. Engagement and support
4. Feedback and continuous improvement

3.3.1.2.1 Welcome and Activation

As the saying goes, "There is never a second chance to create a first impression." For this reason, craft personalized welcome journeys to show appreciation for your customers choosing your services. Send welcome messages via multiple channels—email, SMS, or app notifications—to reach customers on their preferred platform. These messages thank the customer warmly, provide basic account details like their customer ID, and offer initial login instructions.

Also include a brief overview of what to expect next in the onboarding process and introduce customer support options. This reassures customers that assistance is available at every step.
Account activation must be straightforward, with clear, step-by-step instructions:

- **Prepaid customers:** Guidance on inserting the SIM card, activating it via a short code, and setting up voicemail

- **Postpaid customers:** Instructions on logging into the self-service portal, setting up payment methods, and configuring data settings

- **Home services users:** Visual aids for installing broadband equipment, connecting devices, and optimizing Wi-Fi placement

Each step is accompanied by visual aids—diagrams or short videos accessible digitally. Prominently provide a toll-free support line or live chat option so customers can reach out if they encounter issues. This approach eases the process and builds confidence in using your services from day one.

The goal is to make customers feel that *"The activation was so smooth; I was up and running in minutes."*

3.3.1.2.2 Product Education

Product education and usage tips help customers get up to speed. Over the initial month, provide regular educational content, gradually introducing features they may not yet be aware of, for example:

- **Prepaid:** Notifications about bonus data on top-ups and how to use self-care features like data boosts

- **Postpaid:** Emails explaining how to set spending limits and the benefits of e-statements

- **Home services:** Tips on enhancing Wi-Fi security and leveraging cloud storage options

This educational flow is structured and strategically timed, building familiarity without overwhelming the customer. Tools like usage alerts or reminders to explore additional features keep customers engaged at a comfortable pace.

Empower customers by guiding them through self-service options available via your app or online portal. Starting with basic tasks, gradually introduce more advanced features:

- **Prepaid:** Guiding them to check balances, purchase bundles, and access support via unstructured supplementary service data (USSD) codes

- **Postpaid:** Encouraging them to set up automatic payments, view detailed bills, and manage add-ons through the app

- **Home services:** Teaching them to run speed tests, manage connected devices, and schedule support appointments online

By familiarizing customers with these options, they gain autonomy and confidence, reducing the need for customer support.

3.3.1.2.3 Engagement and Support

Use proactive check-ins during the early weeks to ensure customer satisfaction and identify potential issues before they escalate. The first check-in can happen a few days after activation via SMS, email, or a call, asking if everything is working smoothly. A follow-up touchpoint a week later can assess if they need further help.

Each interaction is concise and friendly, providing options to connect with support easily if concerns arise. Proactive check-ins demonstrate your caring approach and commitment to a successful onboarding experience.

Introduce customers to the variety of support channels available, including dedicated support lines, live chat, community forums, and FAQs. By educating customers on the benefits of each support option, they can choose based on their needs and preferred communication style.

Encouraging them to join community forums or social media groups allows them to connect with other users, access tips, and share experiences. This promotes a community atmosphere and adds another layer of engagement beyond formal support channels.

Provide clear information about accessing customer support, with multiple options to suit different preferences. Assure customers that help is readily available and provide estimated response times for each channel. Ensuring that the support process is smooth reinforces the customer's confidence in your service and strengthens their perception of the organization as reliable and customer-focused.

3.3.1.2.4 Feedback and Continuous Improvement

Establish structured feedback mechanisms at critical points, such as after initial setup, at the one-month mark, and after three months. This includes surveys, follow-up calls, or app-based feedback prompts to gather insights on the customer's experience and areas needing improvement.
By monitoring customer usage patterns, you can identify habits or ar-

eas where the customer may benefit from additional support or features:

- **Prepaid:** Notifying customers who frequently top-up about cost-saving bundles

- **Postpaid:** Suggesting plan upgrades for those nearing data limits regularly

- **Home services:** Offering suggestions on optimizing their home setup based on usage spikes

Personalized recommendations help customers get the most out of their plans and increase their perception of your attentiveness to their needs.

Periodically update customers on new features, improvements, and exclusive offers that may enhance their service experience. This includes details on app updates, security enhancements, or seasonal promotions. Consistent, value-oriented updates keep customers informed and show that you are continuously investing in improving their experience.

3.3.1.3 Capabilities

Successful onboarding requires close collaboration among CVM, customer acquisition, product management, assisted inbound channels, and branding teams. While cross-functional collaboration guidelines are outlined in Chapter 5, the onboarding process requires a uniquely deep partnership between CVM and customer acquisition. The CVM team ensures that new customers begin generating revenue, thereby meeting acquisition targets. At the same time, quality acquisitions bolster the customer base and contribute to CVM objectives. However, poorly structured acquisition offers or misaligned customer segments can lead to problems like rotational churn or diluted ARPU. Only continuous, hands-on collaboration—through regular check-ins and information-sharing sessions—can prevent these pitfalls and realize the full potential of onboarding.

From a technology standpoint, automation is key. Welcome messages, product education, and check-in prompts should be triggered automatically whenever customers activate services. This helps to scale effectively and eliminates manual overhead. Most essential capabilities can be delivered with standard CVM technology (see Section 4.3).

Real-time data triggers are particularly important for onboarding. You must be able to identify and act on events like SIM activation, first call, or first recharge as they occur. Accurate data on product usage and billing activity is also necessary to tailor onboarding campaigns and ensure that customers get the most out of their plans.

3.3.1.4 Evaluation

A successful onboarding program yields several tangible benefits:

1. **Reduced early churn:** An increase in the percentage of customers who remain active or continue their contracts beyond the first 90 days

2. **Increased service adoption:** Higher usage of core services, resulting in more top-ups for prepaid or additional upsell opportunities for postpaid

3. **Improved customer satisfaction:** Measurable gains in NPS or other experience metrics, reflecting a positive initial journey

Long-term outcomes include enhanced self-service usage, reduced support costs, and a foundation of trust that paves the way for future cross-sell and upsell initiatives. Typical costs involve program setup, ongoing development of educational materials, and the operational expenses of telemarketing and customer service teams.

3.3.1.5 Summary

Onboarding is the gateway to a long-lasting customer relationship. When executed well, it removes barriers, instills confidence, and cultivates trust. By automating key steps, personalizing communication, and actively seeking feedback, CVM professionals ensure that customers quickly recognize the value of your services. The CVM Canvas below (Figure 3.4) provides an at-a-glance summary of these onboarding elements, offering a unified framework for easy reference and cross-functional alignment.

The Customer Value Management Canvas: **Onboarding Program**

Purpose

Smoothly onboard new postpaid subscribers, encouraging full feature usage, timely bill payments, and early loyalty

Approach

Customer Segments

New postpaid customers (0-90 days lifetime)

Value Delivered

- Quick setup with welcome and activation process
- Easy onboarding to key services
- Proactive support during initial 3 months

Channels

- Email
- SMS
- In-app notifications
- Personalized call center touchpoints.

Capabilites

Technology

Standard CVM technology stack

Data

- Real-time sim activation events
- Accurate data on product usage and billing activity

Collaboration

- Customer acquisition
- Product management
- Assisted inbound channels
- Branding teams

Governance

Monthly steering committee to track progress, resolve issues, and maintain alignment

Evaluation

Gains

- Reduced early churn: An increase in the percentage of customers who continue their contracts beyond the first 90 days
- Increased service adoption: Higher usage of core services, resulting in additional upsell opportunities for postpaid
- Improved customer satisfaction: Measurable gains in NPS or other experience metrics, reflecting a positive initial journey

Costs

- Program setup
- Ongoing development of educational materials
- The operational expenses of telemarketing and customer service teams

Figure 3.4: CVM Canvas for a Postpaid Onboarding Program

3.3.2 Referrals

3.3.2.1 Purpose

The referrals program aims to harness the satisfaction of existing customers to acquire new ones through word-of-mouth recommendations. By turning your customers into brand advocates, you can expand your subscriber base cost-effectively while enhancing customer engagement and loyalty. When customers share positive experiences with friends and family, it leads to higher conversion rates and attracts subscribers who are more likely to stay and generate higher ARPU.

3.3.2.2 Approach

Referrals can be personally sensitive: the referrer stakes their credibility on a recommendation. If the referred individual has a negative experience, the referrer's trustworthiness may suffer. To mitigate this risk and encourage referrals, you must ensure that your customer base has genuinely positive experiences and that the rewards for referring are meaningful enough to justify the personal risk.

When designing a referrals program, three customer segments typically merit special attention:

1. **Loyal advocates:** These customers consistently give high NPS scores and naturally promote your brand. They are motivated by exclusive referral benefits, pride in supporting a brand that aligns with their values, and the intrinsic satisfaction of sharing good experiences.

2. **New customers:** Recently onboarded customers often have fresh enthusiasm for your product and are eager to share their positive impressions. They respond well to incentives similar to loyal advocates, such as exclusive bonuses and recognition for successful referrals.

3. **Price-sensitive customers:** These individuals actively seek ways to reduce costs. They are driven by tangible financial rewards or account credits and will share referral offers if they find the benefit compelling.

Designing a referrals program involves addressing each of these segments with appropriate value propositions. Offers might include exclusive deals for the referrer, social recognition within a loyalty program, or direct monetary rewards such as bill credits.

To ensure that the referrals program is effective and customer-friendly, structure it into four key phases:

1. Incentive design
2. Seamless referral process
3. Promotion and awareness
4. Feedback and continuous improvement

3.3.2.2.1 Incentive Design

Offer compelling incentives that motivate customers to participate. These rewards must appeal to both the referrer and the new customer, creating a win-win situation. Examples include:

- **Discounts on services:** Providing a percentage off the monthly bill for a set period

- **Bonus data or minutes:** Offering additional data or call time to enhance their plan

- **Account credits:** Applying monetary credits to the customer's account

- **Exclusive offers:** Granting access to premium content or services unavailable to others

- **Social recognition:** Creating a special brand community with its events and exclusive activities.

For example, a prepaid customer might receive unlimited data for a month for each successful referral, while the new customer enjoys a discounted starter pack. The goal is to make the rewards attractive enough to encourage customers to refer others enthusiastically.

3.3.2.2.2 Seamless Referral Process

Ensure that the referral process is simple and user-friendly to maximize participation. Key elements include:

- **Multiple channels:** Allowing referrals through SMS, email, social media, or within a mobile app

- **Ease of use:** Providing clear instructions and minimizing the steps required

- **Real-time tracking:** Enabling customers to monitor the status of their referrals and rewards

For example, integrating a referral feature into an app allows customers to send invites directly to their contacts and track their rewards instantly. A straightforward process reduces barriers to participation and enhances the CX.

3.3.2.2.3 Promotion and Awareness

To maximize the program's reach, promote it through various channels:

- **Personalized communications:** Sending targeted SMS campaigns, email newsletters, and in-app notifications

- **Customer touchpoints:** Informing customers about the program during service interactions, on billing statements, and in retail stores

- **Marketing campaigns:** Utilizing mass media channels like television, radio, and online advertising to reach a broader audience

For example, including information about the referral program on monthly bills can prompt postpaid customers to consider referring friends, while in-store signage can capture the attention of prepaid customers.

Continuously monitor the program's performance and make data-driven improvements:

- Tracking KPIs: referral rates, conversion rates, and incremental revenue

- Getting customer feedback through surveys, and support interactions to identify areas for enhancement

- Modifying incentives, communication strategies, or processes based on feedback and data analysis

If data shows that offering bonus data leads to higher referral rates among prepaid customers, you might focus on data incentives in future promotions. Continuous improvement ensures that the program remains effective and relevant.

3.3.2.3 Capabilities

A robust referrals program relies on standard CVM technology (see Section 4.3) for segmentation, offer management, and automated communication. Additionally, specialized systems or modules may be required to track referral activities and seamlessly apply credits or discounts without manual intervention.

Strict adherence to data protection regulations is vital. Both referrers and referees must consent to participation and data sharing. This ensures legal compliance and maintains trust in your brand.

Close teamwork among CVM, product management, branding, marketing, and data analytics teams is essential (see Chapter 5). Continual marketing support is particularly important to keep the referrals program top of mind. Regularly refreshing marketing materials and customizing messages based on different customer segments helps sustain interest and participation.

Monthly steering committees are recommended to evaluate progress, address issues, and adjust tactics. This structured oversight keeps the program aligned with business objectives and ensures a proactive approach to improvements.

3.3.2.4 Evaluation

A well-executed referrals program delivers significant benefits:

- **Increased customer acquisition:** Referrals substantially boost subscriber numbers. Referred customers are more likely to trust your services and convert from prospects to subscribers

- **Lower acquisition costs:** Acquiring customers through referrals is more cost-effective than through traditional marketing channels. The reduced cost per acquisition improves the overall ROI of your marketing efforts. Providing bonus data is often less expensive than extensive advertising campaigns.

- **Enhanced customer engagement and loyalty:** Rewarding customers for referrals strengthens their relationship with you. Engaged customers are less likely to churn and more likely to participate in other CVM programs. A customer who receives account credits for referrals may be more inclined to upgrade to a higher-tier plan.

- **Higher ARPU:** Referred customers often exhibit higher ARPU due to increased trust and engagement. They may be more receptive to additional services like home internet, TV packages, or device upgrades.

However, the program also entails certain costs, such as program setup, referrals technology development and support, rewards delivery, and ongoing marketing activities. Evaluating both sides of the ROI equation—gains versus costs—ensures that the program remains financially and strategically viable.

3.3.2.5 Summary

Referrals are a powerful strategy in the acquire pillar of the CVM Portfolio, leveraging satisfied customers to drive new acquisitions while boosting loyalty and engagement. By offering meaningful rewards, simplifying the referral process, and maintaining rigorous oversight, CVM teams can foster a steady influx of new subscribers at lower cost and with higher lifetime value. Properly executed, referrals strengthen customer advocacy, fuel organic growth, and deliver lasting benefits to both customers and the organization. The CVM Canvas below (Figure 3.5) provides an at-a-glance summary of the most important aspects of referrals program.

The Customer Value Management Canvas:
Referrals Program

Purpose

Leverage existing customers' positive experiences to acquire new subscribers cost-effectively and reinforce loyalty

Approach

Customer Segments

- Loyal advocates who naturally promote the brand
- New customers with fresh enthusiasm for the service
- Price-sensitive users motivated by tangible rewards

Value Delivered

- Exclusive offers for referrers
- Monetary rewards and service discounts for both referrers and referred customers

Channels

- SMS
- Email
- Mobile app

Capabilites

Technology

- Standard CVM platforms
- Specialised referral tracking system

Data

- Price sensitivity scores
- NPS scores
- Referral activity logs
- Consent management

Collaboration

- CVM
- Marketing
- Product management
- IT
- Data analytics

Governance

Monthly steering committees to review performance, maintain data compliance, and drive continuous improvement.

Evaluation

Gains

- Higher customer acquisitions
- Lower cost per acquisition
- Stronger advocacy
- Increased ARPU from referred customers.

Costs

- Referral rewards
- Technology investments into referrals management system
- Ongoing marketing efforts to sustain program visibility and engagement.

Figure 3.5: CVM Canvas for a Referrals Program

3.3.3 Relocations

3.3.3.1 Purpose

Relocations present a unique challenge for telecoms. Even satisfied customers may need to move for work, family, or personal reasons. When relocating, customers effectively become "new" subscribers at their new address, while also ceasing to be customers at their old one. For CVM professionals, this requires viewing relocation as a customer acquisition program—aimed at re-acquiring existing customers who move. The purpose of a relocation program is to ensure that relocating customers can easily continue or upgrade their services at the new address.

3.3.3.2 Approach

Recognize that when a customer relocates, you'll be competing against other telecoms offering signup discounts, free setup, and other benefits. Treat this as a critical touchpoint. It is an opportunity to re-acquire these valuable customers by proactively addressing the challenges they may encounter.

When moving, customers often face several challenges:

- **Service availability issues:** They might find that their current provider doesn't offer coverage at their new address, forcing them to seek alternatives.

- **Unexpected fees:** The move can bring additional costs like transfer fees, activation charges, or increased equipment rental fees, leading to frustration.

- **Contractual complications:** They may encounter early termination fees if the provider can't service the new location or face difficulties transferring bundled services.

- **Service downtime:** Delays in installation or technical issues can result in periods without internet access, which is especially problematic for those who rely on it for work or essential services.

- **Equipment compatibility:** Existing devices like modems or routers may not be compatible at the new location, causing additional expenses or technical difficulties.

While telecoms can't always resolve service availability issues, they can effectively address the other challenges. The relocation program aims to provide a personalized, hassle-free experience for customers moving their services. By ensuring that each move is managed with care, the program helps customers feel valued and supported during a significant life transition.

Organize the relocation program into four phases, each designed to address specific customer challenges:

1. Customer insight and move preparation
2. Personalized service transfer and support
3. Post-move engagement and service optimization
4. Feedback and continuous improvement

3.3.3.2.1 Customer Insight and Move Preparation

3.3.3.2.1.1 Proactive Preparation for Relocation Situations

Predicting which customers are about to relocate is practically impossible for CVM teams. Therefore, it's important to understand the common challenges customers face during relocation, and it's crucial to proactively establish processes that facilitate easy relocation. For example:

- **Contract transfer processes:** Empower the customer service team to transfer existing contracts to the new location without termination or new contract signing fees. Clear procedures should address situations where the new location has incompatible price plans due to different technology, and guidelines should be in place on how to advise customers regarding new devices.

- **Prioritization of existing customers:** Implement processes to prioritize the setup of services for existing customers over new customer acquisitions.

- **Digital relocation services:** Provide digital channels, such as web portals and self-service apps, where customers can request relocation services and find detailed information on how the process works. It's essential to inform customers that this service is available.

- **Upsell and cross-sell recommendations:** Ensure that customer service agents are prepared to offer additional upsell and cross-sell services that might be beneficial in the new location.

These proactive preparations minimize last-minute disruptions and allow for a smooth transition, making the customer feel prioritized and reducing the risk of contractual complications.

3.3.3.2.1.2 Personalized Move Options and Eligibility Check

When a customer notifies you of their move, address all five main challenges:

- **Service availability check:** Verify service availability at the new location to address potential service availability issues.

- **Optimal contract transfer:** Find the best way to transfer the customer's existing contract to the new location. This might involve moving the customer with the same contract or upgrading their plan. For example, a customer with a high-speed broadband plan may be offered the fastest available service at their new address to prevent any downgrade in service quality.

- **Transparent relocation process:** Help customers understand the relocation setup process, ensuring that they experience minimal unexpected fees.

- **Equipment compatibility solutions:** Recommend appropriate equipment options based on the customer's context. Options include retaining existing devices, upgrading to newer models, or adding enhancements like Wi-Fi extenders. Provide easy instructions for self-service installation or schedule a technician visit if needed, ensuring compatibility without unnecessary costs or technical difficulties.

- **Seamless scheduling:** Offer a streamlined, automated process for scheduling the move. Customers can select convenient dates and receive reminders, helping to reduce service downtime.

This comprehensive approach ensures that all challenges associated with relocation are effectively addressed, enhancing the CX.

3.3.3.2.2 Personalized Service Transfer and Support

3.3.3.2.2.1 Proactive Communication and Status Updates

To prevent service downtime and alleviate frustration from delays, maintain proactive communication throughout the moving process. Personalized updates on key milestones—such as equipment shipment, technician arrival reminders, or service activation alerts—are sent via the customer's preferred channels like SMS, email, or in-app messages. This keeps customers informed and reassured, reducing the need for inquiries and building trust in your reliability.

3.3.3.2.2.2 Dedicated Move Support Team and Escalation Pathways

To resolve contractual complications and any issues quickly, assign customers to a dedicated support team trained in move-related queries. This team provides responsive support and has direct escalation pathways for complex cases. By offering knowledgeable assistance, you enhance the customer's confidence that any problems will be swiftly addressed, reinforcing a positive experience even if minor complications arise.

3.3.3.2.3 Post-Move Engagement and Service Optimization

3.3.3.2.3.1 Welcome and Personalized Post-Move Assistance

After the move, send a personalized welcome message to acknowledge the successful transition and express gratitude for the customer's continued loyalty. Provide tips for optimizing their service in the new location—such as router placement for stronger Wi-Fi or adjusting settings for optimal performance. If the new area offers enhanced network capabilities, highlight relevant upgrades or added features, demonstrating your commitment to enhancing their experience.

3.3.3.2.3.2 Service Optimization and Relevant Offers

After analyzing post-move usage patterns, offer tailored recommendations to address any new needs. For example, if a customer's data usage increases in the new location, you might suggest a higher-tier plan or offer a special upgrade to enhance their experience. Also identify customers who may benefit from add-ons like Wi-Fi extenders or enhanced entertainment bundles, presenting these options as supportive solutions rather than promotions.

3.3.3.2.3.3 Proactive Support and Satisfaction Check-Ins

To ensure ongoing satisfaction and prevent future service downtime or contractual issues, conduct proactive check-ins after the move. Through a quick call, SMS, or email, invite customers to share feedback and report any problems. This demonstrates attentiveness and encourages open communication, showing that you are invested in their smooth transition. Use any feedback to refine your services, enhancing the experience for future relocating customers.

3.3.3.2.4 Feedback and Continuous Improvement

3.3.3.2.4.1 Collecting Customer Feedback on the Moving Process

Actively gather feedback to understand how well you've addressed the customer's challenges during the move. Focusing on areas like communication clarity, ease of setup, equipment handling, and overall satisfaction, use in-app surveys or follow-up calls to collect this information. This helps you identify any recurring pain points—such as unexpected fees or equipment issues—that need attention.

3.3.3.2.4.2 Data-Driven Analysis and Adjustments

Using the collected feedback and performance metrics, continuously refine the program to better address customer challenges. For example, if delays in equipment delivery are causing service downtime, work with logistics to streamline this step. If self-service setup options are well-received and reduce technical issues, enhance these resources. These data-driven adjustments allow you to adapt the program dynamically, ensuring a more efficient and customer-friendly moving process.

3.3.3.2.4.3 Long-Term Program Evolution

Regularly evaluate success metrics like post-move retention rates and customer satisfaction scores to assess overall effectiveness. Based on long-term trends, introduce initiatives like reduced installation fees during peak moving seasons to alleviate unexpected costs. By keeping the program responsive to customer needs and market trends, you'll strengthen your reputation for supporting customers through significant life changes.

3.3.3.3 Capabilities

Relocation programs generally rely on standard CVM tools (see Section 4.3). Minor CRM or billing system updates may be needed to accommodate quick and simple contract transfers.

Collaboration among CVM, product management, and assisted inbound channels is critical (see Chapter 5). Customer service teams provide front-line support and help customers to find the optimal solution for relocation, while product management ensures that the underlying systems can manage service changes without disruptions. Regular steering committees—monthly or quarterly—help track program performance and resolve issues.

From a data perspective, accurate service availability information and clear timelines for network expansions are essential. Customers who discover that your network will soon be available in their new location may be willing to wait and avoid switching providers.

3.3.3.4 Evaluation

A well-executed relocation program can yield measurable benefits:

- **Reduced involuntary churn:** Streamlined relocation keeps satisfied customers in your base instead of losing them due to coverage gaps or complicated contract transfers.

- **Increased service revenue:** Relocation often uncovers upsell opportunities, such as higher-tier plans or new product bundles.

- **Higher customer satisfaction:** Positive experiences increase loyalty, reflected in metrics like NPS or customer effort scores.

Costs include the initial launch of the program, possible technician visits, and any revenue losses if a plan downgrades at the new location. By comparing these expenses against churn reduction and incremental ARPU, CVM professionals can determine the overall ROI.

3.3.3.5 Summary

Relocation is not merely a technical transfer of services, it is a critical CVM initiative that treats a customer's move as a re-acquisition opportunity. By anticipating relocation issues, offering transparent processes, and responding with agility, telecoms ensure that satisfied customers seamlessly transition to their new homes. Successful relocation programs reduce churn, uncover new revenue streams, and strengthen the customer relationship during a pivotal life event. The CVM Canvas below (Figure 3.6) provides a simple summary of a relocations program.

The Customer Value Management Canvas:
Relocations Program

Purpose

Retain customers who move by streamlining contract transfers and offering relevant upgrades, preventing involuntary churn

Approach

Customer Segments

Any existing home service customers planning to relocate

Value Delivered

- Seamless service continuation
- Transparent fees
- Proactive support to simplify moving

Channels

- Inbound assisted channels

Capabilites

Technology

- Standard CVM technology stack
- Minor CRM and billing system upgrades that allow quick contract transfers

Data

- Accurate coverage information
- Move notifications
- Real-time feedback to tailor offers and address issues promptly

Collaboration

- CVM
- Product management
- IT
- Customer service team

Governance

Monthly or quarterly reviews to track relocation metrics, solve operational issues, and refine processes.

Evaluation

Gains

- Reduced involuntary churn
- Higher ARPU of relocated customers
- Improved relocated customers satisfaction

Costs

- Initial program setup
- Technician visits
- System enhancements
- Any potential revenue loss from plan downgrades.

Figure 3.6: CVM Canvas for a Relocations Program

3.3.4 Prepaid-to-Postpaid Migration

3.3.4.1 Purpose

Prepaid-to-Postpaid (Pre2Post) programs aim to convert value-seeking prepaid customers into stable, higher-spend postpaid subscribers. This transition not only boosts ARPU but also paves the way for cross-selling services that can deepen the customer's relationship with the telecom. Customers benefit from greater convenience, enhanced services, and predictable billing, while the telecom gains a more reliable revenue stream and improved customer loyalty.

However, the Pre2Post migration program often sparks internal debates due to inherent complexities:

- **Revenue shifts:** High-value prepaid customers transitioning to postpaid can dilute prepaid revenue, causing conflicts between prepaid and postpaid teams.

- **Short-term revenue impact:** Postpaid plans may offer more value at a lower cost compared to prepaid packages, potentially leading to an initial drop in overall revenue. For example, prepaid customers purchasing multiple high-value data packages might spend more than they would on an unlimited postpaid plan.

- **Increased credit risk:** Postpaid services depend on customers' ability to pay monthly bills, introducing credit risk absent in prepaid models.

- **Customer resistance:** Prepaid customers often value flexibility and control over expenses, exhibiting resistance to switching to postpaid plans.

For this reason, the decision to implement a Pre2Post migration program or not should be based on the specific context of the telecom.

3.3.4.2 Approach

Moving from a pay-as-you-go model to a monthly subscription is a significant behavioral shift. Many prepaid customers prefer flexibility, transparency, and the absence of credit checks. Postpaid offers greater convenience, loyalty rewards, and the potential for bundled discounts, but it also includes monthly bills that must be paid on time. A successful Pre2Post migration program addresses these concerns through three key strategies:

1. Precise customer identification and segmentation
2. Tailored offers
3. Retention-focused onboarding process

3.3.4.2.1 Precise Customer Identification and Segmentation

Accurate identification and segmentation of potential postpaid customers are crucial. Leveraging ML models enhances this process by analyzing extensive customer data to predict behavior more precisely. Instead of merely predicting which customers are likely to convert, the focus is on identifying those who will convert and remain active, and who will pay bills on time over an extended period.

Key data inputs for predictive models include:

- **Demographics:** Age, device type, location, and other attributes influencing purchasing power and payment reliability

- **Usage patterns:** Average recharge frequency and data and voice consumption trends over 90-day and 180-day periods, indicating engagement levels

- **Financial transactions:** Mobile financial services usage, offering insights into financial behavior and creditworthiness

- **Recharge history:** Historical spending patterns and commitment levels, reflecting loyalty and potential for higher-value plans

Employing financial analytics to assess creditworthiness mitigates the risk associated with postpaid billing, ensuring that only customers with reliable recharge histories are targeted.

3.3.4.2.2 Tailored Offers

Personalizing offers to each customer's specific needs increases acceptance rates and enhances satisfaction. Utilizing next best offer (NBO) recommendations ensures that proposed postpaid plans align with customers' usage patterns and preferences.

Strategies for crafting targeted NBOs include:

- **Personalized plan recommendations:** Propose postpaid plans that match or slightly exceed the customer's average monthly recharges while offering additional benefits. For example, if a customer consistently recharges $30 per month for data packs, offer a postpaid plan slightly above this amount with more data than they get on prepaid plans.

- **Financial risk assessment:** Prioritize offers based on the customer's financial capabilities to minimize credit risk.

3.3.4.2.3 Retention-Focused Onboarding Process

Transitioning from prepaid to postpaid represents a significant behavioral shift. A seamless onboarding process ensures that customers adapt comfortably to their new plans and remain engaged long-term.

Key components of the onboarding process include:

- **Personalized welcome:** Send automated messages acknowledging the customer's choice and highlighting the benefits of their new postpaid plan, such as enhanced services or exclusive offers.

- **Account setup assistance:** Provide clear guides for activating the plan, managing payments, and utilizing self-service options within the app.

- **Educational content:** Offer tips on maximizing plan features, including data rollover, international roaming, and understanding the billing cycle. Emphasize the convenience of postpaid services compared to prepaid.

- **Invoice management:** Educate customers on receiving and paying invoices, highlighting multiple payment options and the ease of automatic payments.

- **Usage monitoring:** Continuously analyze usage patterns to identify customers at risk of churn, allowing for proactive engagement and support.

- **Personalized recommendations:** Suggest plan adjustments or add-ons based on evolving needs, such as international calling packs for customers making frequent overseas calls.

- **Feedback collection:** Conduct surveys to gather insights and improve the migration process, demonstrating a commitment to customer satisfaction.

Focusing on retention from the outset builds customer loyalty and reduces churn, maximizing the long-term benefits of the migration program.

3.3.4.3 Capabilities

Pre2Post migration programs rely on the standard CVM toolkit (see Section 4.3), with an emphasis on machine learning models and NBO engines. Advanced analytics enable precise segmentation and credit risk scoring, ensuring that only the most suitable prepaid customers receive migration offers.

Minor updates to IT or CRM systems may be required to streamline the migration process, allowing customers to keep the same number as they move to a postpaid plan.

Strong collaboration between prepaid and postpaid teams is essential to prevent internal friction. Assisted inbound channels (see Section 5.8)—such as call centers, retail stores, and digital platforms—must offer a smooth and consistent migration experience. Monthly steering meetings with all involved functions are recommended to maintain alignment and track program performance.

Accurate usage data, credit scores, and migration logs are vital for refining these campaigns. By feeding performance metrics back into ML models, CVM teams can enhance predictive accuracy and optimize future offers.

3.3.4.4 Evaluation

A well-structured Pre2Post program yields benefits in both revenue and customer satisfaction:

- **Higher ARPU:** Postpaid subscribers typically spend more than prepaid users, partly due to predictable billing cycles and bundled services.

- **Improved loyalty:** Postpaid customers often display higher retention rates, creating a stable base for cross-selling services like home internet or TV.

- **Expanded cross-sell opportunities:** After building trust, operators can promote additional products, ranging from device upgrades to premium service bundles.

Typical costs and risks include initial program setup, potential short-term revenue dips (if some prepaid customers opt for lower postpaid plans than their historical prepaid spend), and an increase in bad debts if credit checks are insufficient or misapplied. Continual monitoring of financial metrics helps balance these risks against the longer-term advantages of a larger postpaid base.

3.3.4.5 Summary

Pre2Post migration expands acquire strategies in the CVM Portfolio, driving sustainable growth by converting prepaid subscribers into higher-value postpaid customers. Success depends on precise targeting, data-driven segmentation, and a seamless onboarding process. By aligning teams, employing robust analytics, and offering compelling postpaid propositions, telecoms can create loyal relationships that go beyond simple subscriptions. CVM Canvas below (see Figure 3.7) provides a summary view of the program.

The Customer Value Management Canvas:
Pre2Post Migration Program

Purpose

Increase ARPU and customer loyalty by transitioning high-potential prepaid users to postpaid plans

Approach

Customer Segments

- Prepaid customers who are likely to move to postpaid
- And have low credit risk scores

Value Delivered

- Better value for money (more data for the same price)
- Convenience of being never cut of due to empty balance
- Extra postpaid perks

Channels

- Assisted outbound channels
- Assisted inbound channels

Capabilites

Technology

- Standard CVM technology stack
- Machine learning models
- Next-best-offer engine
- CRM and billing system enhancements

Data

- Usage frequency
- Recharge patterns
- Credit risk assessments
- Mobile financial services history

Collaboration

- Close coordination among prepaid, postpaid CVM teams
- IT
- Data analytics
- Assisted channels

Governance

Monthly steering meetings with clear KPIs, cross-functional updates, and decision-making checkpoints.

Evaluation

Gains

- Higher ARPU
- Improved Loyalty
- Expanded Cross-Sell Opportunities

Costs

- Program setup expenses
- Potential short-term revenue declines
- Risk of increased number of bad debts

Figure 3.7: CVM Canvas for a Prepaid-to-Postpaid Migration Program

3.4 Grow

The second CVM Portfolio pillar is "grow" and it groups initiatives related to existing customer growth. To consistently deliver value to customers and maximize CLV, the grow pillar emphasizes strategies designed to expand the share of value provided to existing customers over time. At the core of this approach are upsell, cross-sell, and loyalty programs, which are carefully crafted to offer products and services that genuinely enhance customers' experiences while driving incremental revenue and profitability for the telecom.

 **3.4.1 Upsell**

3.4.1.1 Purpose

The primary goal of an upsell program is to increase the value customers receive from your core services. It goes beyond merely raising prices; it involves carefully crafted strategies that stimulate higher usage, deliver improved quality, or bundle multiple services under a "more-for-more" framework. By addressing genuine customer needs, these initiatives strengthen relationships with existing subscribers and foster long-term revenue growth.

Examples of common upsell strategies include:

- **Price adjustments** (common in many European markets during the COVID-19 pandemic)

- **Boosting service consumption** (e.g., offering free data for a week with top-ups exceeding a predefined threshold)

- **Enhancing service quality** (e.g., migrating customers to 5G)

- **Packaging multiple services** (e.g., bundling voice, data, and entertainment at a discounted rate)

Each approach works best under specific conditions and market dynamics. However, all successful strategies share the same principle: providing meaningful value to customers in exchange for higher spend.

3.4.1.2 Approach

3.4.1.2.1 Prepaid

There are many tactics on how to upsell prepaid customers, but we will focus on two fundamental upsell opportunities—reducing customers' time in out-of-balance situations and increasing consumption.

3.4.1.2.1.1 Reducing Customers' Time Out-of-Balance

Regular prepaid customers typically have stable communication needs. Upsell capacity lies in the missed potential when customers wish to use services (voice, SMS, data) but lack sufficient balance—whether due to depleted core balance, exhausted package limits, or expired packages—and are consequently cut off from outgoing services. The periods when customers are disconnected represent lost revenue potential for the telecom. The greater the percentage of time customers are out-of-balance, the larger the upsell opportunity.

To address this, the optimal upsell strategy involves implementing initiatives that minimize customers' cut-off time. Potential solutions include:

- Offering larger packages to extend usage periods

- Promoting longer-duration packages to reduce the frequency of top-ups

- Enabling auto-recharges from postpaid accounts or credit cards to prevent service interruptions

- Providing microcredits that offer temporary core balances or packages

- Incentivizing more frequent or larger top-ups through bonuses or rewards

- Migrating prepaid customers to postpaid plans to ensure uninterrupted service

3.4.1.2.1.2 Increasing Consumption with a More-for-More Strategy

Another effective upsell strategy is to incentivize customers to purchase slightly more in exchange for greater value, similar to the pricing tactics used by businesses like McDonald's, where a larger meal costs only slightly more than a medium one, encouraging customers to opt for the larger size.

In prepaid services, this strategy can be applied by:

- **Incentivizing larger top-ups:** Identifying the regular top-up amounts that customers typically add and offering bonuses when they top up 30 percent more than their usual amount.

- **Promoting larger packages:** Presenting package options where the first choice is slightly more expensive but provides significantly more value, encouraging customers to choose the higher-tier package. Higher tier might mean more data, or more extra services like unlimited social media platforms, or gaming sites.

3.4.1.2.1.3 Optimal Timing for Upselling Initiatives

The best moments to initiate upsell efforts are when specific customer signals occur:

- **Low account balance thresholds:** When customers' balances drop below a certain amount, they can be prompted with top-up offers or auto-recharge options to prevent service disruption.

- **Low package balance thresholds:** As customers approach depletion of their data, voice, or SMS balances, immediate add-ons and upgrades can be offered to maintain service continuity.

- **Impending package expiration:** Timely reminders and renewal incentives can be effective when a customer's package is about to expire, encouraging them to renew or upgrade their package.

3.4.1.2.2 Postpaid

In postpaid services, two fundamental upsell strategies prevail: increasing consumption through more-for-more offerings and promoting device renewals and upgrades.

3.4.1.2.2.1 Increasing Consumption with More-for-More Offerings

This principle mirrors that of prepaid services: present customers with price plan options where a slightly higher cost delivers significantly more value, encouraging them to opt for higher-tier plans. However, postpaid services face unique challenges.

First, telecoms often offer a limited number of price plans—sometimes as few as three—for the entire customer base. While this simplifies choices for new customers, it restricts upsell opportunities among existing subscribers. Addressing this limitation may require rethinking the business strategy to introduce more varied or customizable plans.

Second, when a majority of postpaid customers are already on unlimited plans with no higher tiers available, upselling becomes challenging. In such cases, product innovation is essential. Introducing new offerings like capped 5G plans, family bundles, or convergence services can create fresh opportunities to enhance customer value and drive revenue growth.

Recommending the NBO is usually straightforward: telecoms need to analyze existing customer data usage and match it with optimal price plan options.

3.4.1.2.2.2 Promoting Device Renewals and Upgrades

Mobile devices have predictable life cycles; for example, customers replace iPhones every three to five years and other brands every two to four years. As many telecom markets have shifted from subsidizing devices to offering device leasing options, opportunities for device renewals and upgrades have increased, along with complementary products like device insurance.

Each new generation of devices offers enhanced features and capabilities, typically leading to increased data consumption. Although device renewal cycles are not directly tied to mobile price plans, they significantly impact plan usage and revenue.

Unlike price plan recommendations, suggesting appropriate device upgrades involves more complexity. Brand loyalty plays a significant role, for example—approximately four out of five iPhone users upgrade to a new iPhone. Other customers may prefer devices that are on sale during their renewal period. To effectively recommend devices, telecoms need to employ ML algorithms to analyze customer preferences and predict the best device matches.

3.4.1.2.2.3 Optimal Timing for Upselling Initiatives

Identifying the right moment is crucial for successful upselling in postpaid services:

- **Approaching data allowance limits:** Customers nearing or exceeding their data limits can be encouraged to upgrade to higher-tier plans.

- **Contract or offer expiration:** Proactive engagement as contracts or special offers approach their end dates can secure renewals or plan upgrades.

- **Device lease termination:** Offering new device deals to customers whose device leases are concluding can stimulate upgrades and renewals.

- **Service interactions:** When customers seek device servicing or support, presenting upgrade options can capitalize on their engagement with the brand.

- **New device purchase:** When customers purchase new devices it's perfect timing to offer a price plan upgrade as well.

3.4.1.2.3 Home services

Home services—comprising broadband internet, television, and landline telephony—offer substantial opportunities for upselling through more-for-more strategies and by capitalizing on distinctive customer behaviors and signals.

Encourage customers to opt for higher-tier plans by presenting options where a slightly higher cost delivers significantly more value. For example, offering higher broadband speeds for an incremental price increase appeals to customers seeking enhanced performance. Similarly, adding premium television packages, extra set-top boxes, or advanced home phone features can incentivize customers to upgrade their existing services.

What sets home services apart is the variety of unique occasions and signals that present upselling opportunities.

When new technologies like fiber-optic internet become available at a customer's address, offering an upgrade can significantly enhance their service experience while increasing ARPU. Detecting an increase in connected devices through network monitoring indicates a need for higher bandwidth packages, prompting an upsell initiative.

Major sporting events such as the Olympics or the World Cup often drive demand for premium sports channels or high-definition broadcasts, offering timely opportunities to promote relevant upgrades. Additionally, customers who frequently purchase on-demand content like movies or shows could be offered subscription-based services such as HBO or Netflix integrations, adding value and convenience.

When customers relocate to a new residence, it presents an ideal time to propose service enhancements, such as faster internet options or tailored bundled services.

To effectively recommend the NBO, leveraging data analytics and ML algorithms is essential. By analyzing customer behavior, preferences, and usage patterns, you can predict potential needs and generate personalized recommendations that resonate with individual customers.

3.4.1.3 Capabilities

An effective upsell program depends on a structured rollout that aligns technical, data, and people capabilities. As illustrated in Figure 3.8, the process generally follows seven stages:

- **Analysis and business case:** Define upsell objectives and assess potential ROI. Identify prerequisites such as data availability and system readiness to evaluate how much incremental ARPU the initiative could generate.

- **Integration and channel alignment:** Ensure the appropriate channels (e.g., SMS, email, app notifications, retail, call centers) and systems (billing, CRM, CMS) are equipped to support the upsell use case. Document technical requirements for easy reference. Collaboration that is unusual in upsell is alignment with device logistics team, because it requires making sure that we are promoting devices that are available for customers to purchase.

- **Data preparation and management:** Standardize data definitions and prepare accurate inputs for segmentation and ML models. Establish automated data flows for real-time responsiveness.

- **Customer segmentation and profiling:** Use usage patterns, churn risk, and offer responsiveness to define target segments. ML models help identify which customers are most likely to accept specific offers.

- **Next best offer recommendation:** Match each segment to the most relevant upsell. Personalization increases acceptance rates by ensuring offers are closely aligned with customer needs.

- **Communication and engagement:** Coordinate outbound messages (SMS, email, app notifications) and inbound interactions (call centers, self-service portals) for consistent, real-time engagement.

- **Monitoring, Reporting, and Continuous Improvement:** Set up dashboards to track metrics like incremental revenue and churn reduction. Adjust offers based on performance insights to enhance results over time.

STAGE	ACTIVITIES	DELIVERABLE
Analysis and Business Case	• Business requirement analysis • Business case evaluation • Solution design • Prerequisites identification	Detailed solution design
Integration and Channel Alignment	• Identification of needed integration and channels • Specification and solution designs alignment with technicians	Requirements for integration
Data Preparation and Management	• Data definitions alignment • Testing and cleaning • Integrating with CMS	Automated data flow to CMS
Customer Segmentation and Profiling	• Customer base analysis or segmentation for signal definition • ML/AI model	Customer base/target base segments
Next Best Offer Recommendation	• Best offer/message identification	Personalized offer assignment for each of the actions
Communication and Engagement	• Configuration of the campaign in outbound channels • Communication of campaign in inbound channels	Automated campaigns running and targeting clients
Monitoring, Reporting, and Continuous Improvement	• Data preparation for reporting • Reporting set up	Daily reporting for business results track

Figure 3.8: Seven Stages Supporting a CVM Upsell Program Implementation

Upsell is an extremely cross-functional program, so close collaboration among CVM, product management, pricing, and channel teams, and IT is crucial (see Chapter 5). Regular governance meetings—weekly or monthly—keep all stakeholders aligned, highlight operational issues early, and ensure continuous optimization.

On the technology side, the standard CVM stack (see Section 4.3) is a prerequisite. Customer data management, ML-driven targeting, NBO solutions, and campaign management systems form the backbone of an automated, data-driven upsell capability. Real-time analytics enable immediate reactions to customer signals, driving higher conversion rates and better CX.

3.4.1.4 Evaluation

When executed properly, upsell programs drive three primary benefits:

- **Growing ARPU:** Higher-tier packages, additional services, or premium bundles lead to increased revenue per user.

- **Increased usage:** Enhanced devices, faster broadband, or additional features all stimulate consumption.

- **Reduced churn:** By continuously delivering new value, telecoms retain satisfied customers.

Against these gains, operators incur setup and operating costs:

- **Program setup:** System integrations, data cleansing, configuration of ML models, and staff training

- **Ongoing assisted channel costs:** Telemarketing and other channel incentives

- **Sales bonuses:** Commissions to frontline teams for successful upsell conversions

Balancing these costs against incremental revenue forms the basis for ROI calculations and helps refine program strategies over time.

3.4.1.5 Summary

Upselling represents one of the most direct ways to grow revenue from an existing customer base. By carefully analyzing usage patterns, detecting signals of increased demand or device upgrade opportunities, and delivering personalized offers at the right times, CVM professionals can steadily expand average revenue while improving customer satisfaction. Seamless collaboration between technology, product, and channel teams—and a commitment to ongoing measurement and refinement—are the key drivers of an effective upsell program. The CVM Canvas in Figure 3.9 provides a summary view of upsell program for prepaid.

The Customer Value Management Canvas:
Prepaid Upsell Program

Purpose

Grow prepaid customers ARPU by reducing customers' time in out-of-balance situations and increasing consumption

Approach

Customer Segments

Prepaid users with frequent out-of-balance situations, or demonstrated potential for increased consumption.

Value Delivered

- Longer uninterrupted service with microcredits and lend me balance products
- Better prices for larger data bundles
- Significant bonus on larger top-ups

Channels

- SMS
- USSD
- In-app notifications
- Inbound assisted channels

Capabilites

Technology

- Customer data platform
- Campaign management system
- Next best offer recommendations
- Machine learning algorithms
- Reporting

Data

- Account balance threshold events
- Top-up frequency events
- Propensity for upsell
- Credit risk
- Usage behavior

Collaboration

- CVM
- IT
- Data analytics
- Product management
- Inbound and outbound channels

Governance

Weekly cross-functional check-ins to review performance metrics, refine offers, and resolve operational issues.

Evaluation

Gains

- Growing ARPU: Higher-tier packages, additional services, or premium bundles lead to increased revenue per user
- Increased Usage: Enhanced devices, faster broadband, or additional features all stimulate consumption
- Reduced Churn: By continuously delivering new value, telecoms retain satisfied customers

Costs

- Program Setup: System integrations, data cleansing, configuration of ML models, and staff training
- Ongoing Assisted Channel Costs: Telemarketing and other channel incentives
- Sales Bonuses: Commissions to frontline teams for successful upsell conversions.

Figure 3.9: CVM Canvas for a Prepaid Upsell Program

3.4.2 Core Services Cross-sell

3.4.2.1 Purpose

Cross-selling core services focuses on enriching each customer's experience by consolidating multiple telecom services—mobile, broadband, TV, and more—into a single provider relationship. This strategy not only boosts revenue by increasing ARPU but it also deepens customer loyalty and reduces churn. When executed effectively, cross-selling core services drives significant growth while enhancing the overall customer experience.

Core services cross-selling programs often yield the most significant impact among growth initiatives because they generate substantial additional revenue and strengthen customer relationships. Research supports the effectiveness of cross-selling in reducing churn. For example, a study that synthesized findings from 37 articles published between 1999 and 2022 noted that customers who adopt fully converged solutions—integrated service packages combining multiple offerings—tend to exhibit much higher loyalty (Ribeiro et al., 2023). This increased retention is attributed to the added value and convenience of bundled services, which enhance customer satisfaction and create higher switching costs.

3.4.2.2 Approach

3.4.2.2.1 Transitioning from Subscription-centric to Household-centric Analysis

Traditionally, telecoms have analyzed cross-selling opportunities from a subscription perspective, focusing on individual services like single mobile lines or broadband connections (see Figure 3.10). This approach limits our understanding of customers' broader needs and overlooks opportunities to offer additional services that could enhance their experience. By concentrating solely on subscriptions, we miss the interconnectedness of services within a household, where multiple users and devices coexist.

Family uses 8 digital services and spends $184 per month

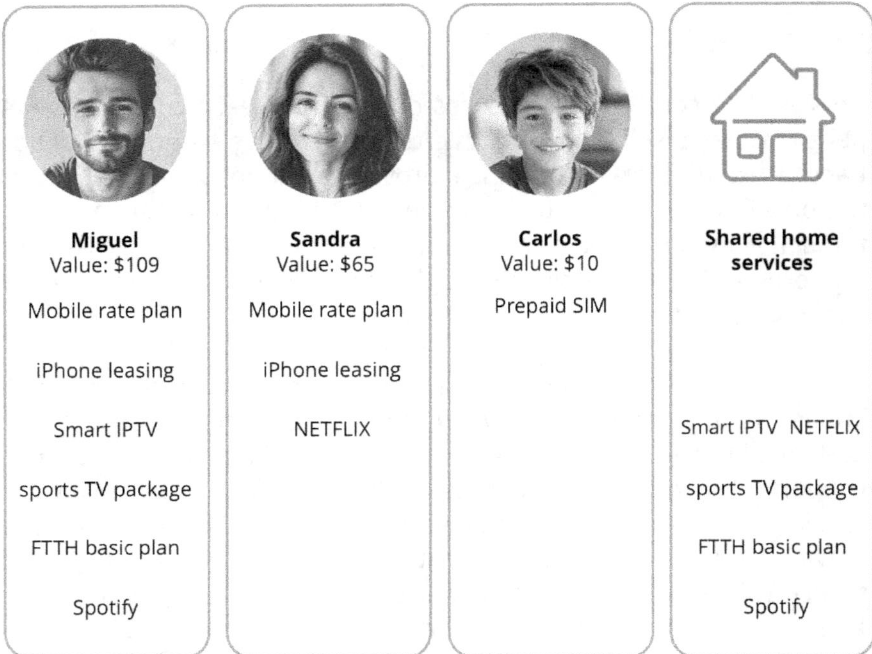

Figure 3.10: Examples of How Different Household Members Sign Subscription Contracts

Analyzing only from a subscription perspective presents several gaps (see Figure 3.11):

- **Limited visibility of customer needs:** Without considering household dynamics, we fail to see how services can complement each other, such as bundling mobile and home internet services.

- **Missed bundling opportunities:** Overlooking the household perspective means missing chances to offer packages that provide added value and convenience.

- **Inefficient marketing efforts:** Targeting individuals rather than households can lead to fragmented campaigns that do not fully capitalize on potential revenue streams.

This is how telecom sees this family from subscription perspective

Subscription #1
- Name: Miguel
- Value: $55
- Services: Mobile rate plan, iPhone leasing

Subscription #2
- Name: Miguel
- Value: $45
- Services: Smart IPTV plan, sports TV package, fiber basic plan

Subscription #3
- Name: Miguel
- Value: $9
- Services: Spotify premium

Subscription #4
- Name: Sandra
- Value: $55
- Services: Mobile rate plan, iPhone leasing

Subscription #5
- Name: Sandra
- Value: $10
- Services: Netflix

Subscription #6
- Name: Carlos
- Value: $10
- Services: Prepaid SIM

Figure 3.11: Examples of Subscription-centric Analysis

By shifting to a household-centric perspective, you significantly expand your cross-selling opportunities (see Figure 3.12). Viewing customers as households allows you to:

- **Identify service gaps:** Determine which services each household currently uses and which ones they lack.

- **Assess market potential:** Count all households in your service area and determine your service penetration within them to estimate the total market.

- **Tailor offers to household needs:** Develop personalized bundles that address the specific requirements of each household, making your offerings more attractive.

For example, many telecoms discover that only a minority of households in their market use converged solutions from a single provider. This fact reveals a substantial untapped potential for growth. Winning a household and providing excellent service can secure long-term customer loyalty.

3.4.2.2.2 Developing Effective Cross-selling Strategies

Understanding this potential allows you to think about cross-selling strategies that aim to win one household at a time. You can list all households and design cross-selling paths for each, then work diligently on executing these plans. Key cross-selling paths include:

- **Mobile to home services:** Offering mobile broadband, fixed broadband, TV packages, and over-the-top services to mobile customers who do not yet use your home services

- **Home services to mobile customers:** Introducing mobile plans to households that currently only subscribe to your fixed broadband or TV services

- **Family plans:** Promoting family mobile plans that encourage all household members to consolidate their mobile services with you

Cross-selling and Upselling from a Household Perspective

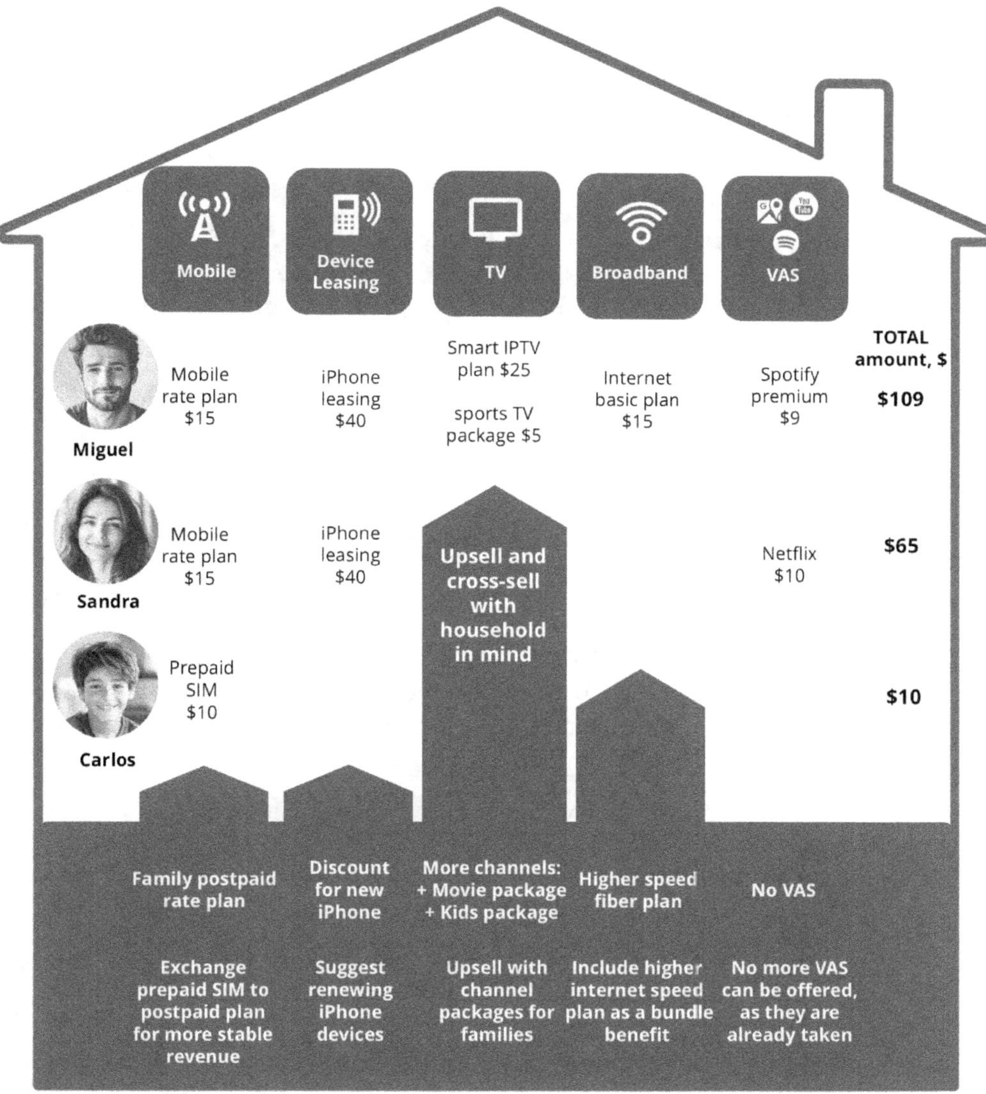

Figure 3.12: Cross-selling and Upselling from a Household Perspective

- **Wearables and internet of things devices:** Offering eSIMs for wearables and IoT devices to existing mobile customers, expanding their ecosystem of connected devices

- **All-in-one packages:** Creating comprehensive bundles that include multiple mobile lines, broadband, and TV services, meeting all communication and entertainment needs of the household

3.4.2.3 Capabilities

To deliver on these cross-selling opportunities, CVM professionals need several foundational capabilities:

- **Household identification and mapping:** Create a reliable view of each household's existing services. You may need to combine internal customer data with external datasets, such as address records or household income information, to build accurate household profiles.

- **Converged product development:** Package multiple services into a single bundle that adds tangible value, such as cost savings, shared data allowances, or streamlined billing. Simple things such as receiving and paying a single bill eliminates a lot of friction for customers.

- **Recommendation algorithms:** Develop predictive models that leverage machine learning to pinpoint which households or segments are most likely to buy additional services. This data-driven approach can greatly improve targeting effectiveness.

- **Omnichannel execution:** Execute cross-selling campaigns across all touchpoints, including online self-service portals, mobile apps, retail stores, contact centers, and in-home technicians. Consistency across channels fosters trust and drives higher conversion rates.

- **Cross-functional collaboration:** Engage product management teams, marketing, IT, customer service, and sales to ensure alignment on offer design, pricing, and customer messaging.

This collaboration streamlines execution and enhances the overall customer experience.

Monthly or quarterly cross-functional check-ins to review performance metrics, refine offers, and resolve operational issues are recommended.

3.4.2.4 Evaluation

Measuring cross-selling outcomes involves tracking both financial and operational KPIs:

- **Increased ARPU:** Expanded service adoption drives higher monthly revenue per user, improving profitability.

- **Reduced churn:** Bundled services raise switching costs and foster deeper engagement, making customers less likely to churn.

- **Elevated customer satisfaction:** Tailored bundles that address household needs boost satisfaction by providing relevant solutions in a single, convenient package.

Costs typically associated with cross-selling include program setup, IT development for converged products, third-party data purchases (for accurate household mapping), and sales commissions. CVM teams must continuously monitor ROI by comparing incremental revenue gains with these expenses, ensuring a sustainable growth strategy.

3.4.2.5 Summary

Cross-selling programs unlock significant growth potential by consolidating multiple services for each household. A household-centric perspective, backed by data-driven segmentation and converged product offerings, boosts ARPU and reduces churn. When properly executed, cross-selling delivers measurable gains in revenue, loyalty, and customer satisfaction—ultimately contributing to a more sustainable and profitable telecom business. The CVM Canvas in Figure 3.13 provides a summary view of a core services cross-sell program.

The Customer Value Management Canvas:
Core Services Cross-sell Program

Purpose

Expand each household's telecom relationship by cross-selling all services relevant for the household

Approach

Customer Segments

- Mobile only customers
- Home services only customers

Value Delivered

- Convenience with a single invoice
- Cost savings with convergence plans
- Enhanced experience by consolidating multiple services under one provider

Channels

- Digital channels (email, in-app, self service)
- Assisted inbound channels (in-store visits, contact centers)
- Assisted outbound channels (telemarketing, in-home technicians)

Capabilites

Technology

- Standard CVM technology stack
- Machine learning algorithms
- Changes in billing platform to support single invoice

Data

- Household information and identity mapping
- Propensity scores to purchase services

Collaboration

- CVM
- Product Management
- Pricing
- IT
- Channels and sales teams

Governance

Cross-functional steering committee to oversee campaign approvals, converged product development, and performance tracking

Evaluation

Gains

- Increased ARPU
- Stronger customer loyalty

Costs

- Initial program setup
- IT development
- Third-party data acquisition
- Sales commissions

Figure 3.13: CVM Canvas for Core Services Cross-sell Program

3.4.3 Value-Added Services Cross-sell

3.4.3.1 Purpose

The primary objective of cross-selling value-added services (VAS) for telecoms is to drive revenue growth and strengthen customer loyalty by introducing relevant, high-value services that complement core telecom offerings. VAS offerings provide additional functionalities and services beyond core voice and data plans, like TV or Music streaming, insurance, credit cards, accessories, etc. While these services often involve third-party products with lower profit margins compared to standard telecom offerings, they may play a crucial role in differentiating the brand and enhancing customer engagement.

Understanding customers' lifestyles and preferences is key. By leveraging behavioral data, telecoms can launch tailored VAS packages that address real customer needs—whether that involves fitness trackers for health-conscious users or roaming bundles for frequent travelers. This alignment between telecom capabilities and customer lifestyles builds goodwill, boosts service adoption, and positions the telecom as a valuable partner in everyday life.

3.4.3.2 Approach

Telecoms must shift from acting solely as network providers to operating more like e-commerce platforms when cross-selling VAS. The sheer volume of potential products requires a methodical approach anchored in data insights, personalization, and strategic partnerships. For mobile customers, typical VAS offerings may include:

- **Premium content subscriptions:** Access to streaming services like Netflix, HBO, or Disney+, music platforms such as Spotify or Deezer, and audiobook services like Audible

- **Discounted international calling bundles:** Special rates for international calls catering to customers with family or business connections abroad

- **Roaming packages:** Data and voice packages for frequent travelers, ensuring seamless connectivity while abroad

- **Financial services:** Mobile wallets, microloans, insurance products, and payment solutions integrated into the mobile experience

- **Lifestyle apps and services:** Health and fitness apps, mobile gaming subscriptions, navigation services, and cloud storage solutions

- **Device add-ons:** Accessories like earbuds, smartwatches, portable chargers, and protective cases offered at promotional prices

For home service customers, VAS may include:

- **Smart home solutions:** Home security systems, automation devices, energy management tools, and smart appliances that integrate with broadband services

- **Advanced Wi-Fi solutions:** Mesh Wi-Fi systems, Wi-Fi extenders, and enhanced routers for improved home connectivity

- **Streaming services bundles:** Combining broadband with subscriptions to premium TV channels, video-on-demand platforms, and OTT services

- **Home entertainment devices:** Offering smart TVs, set-top boxes, gaming consoles, and sound systems as part of the home service package

A critical success factor is leveraging analytics to segment customers based on behavior, preferences, and lifestyles. By identifying these distinct groups, you can create targeted VAS bundles and deliver them through inbound and outbound channels at precisely the right time. Although VAS offerings compete with countless specialized market players, you as a telecom possess one significant advantage: extensive customer data and direct customer relationships.

Lifestyle-based bundling illustrates the power of this data-driven approach:

- **Fitness enthusiasts:** Bundling wearable devices like fitness trackers or smartwatches with health and fitness apps, music streaming services for workouts, and mobile data plans suitable for outdoor activities (see Figure 3.14)

There is opportunity to create more value for consumers by packaging offers to fully meet their Digital Lifestyles

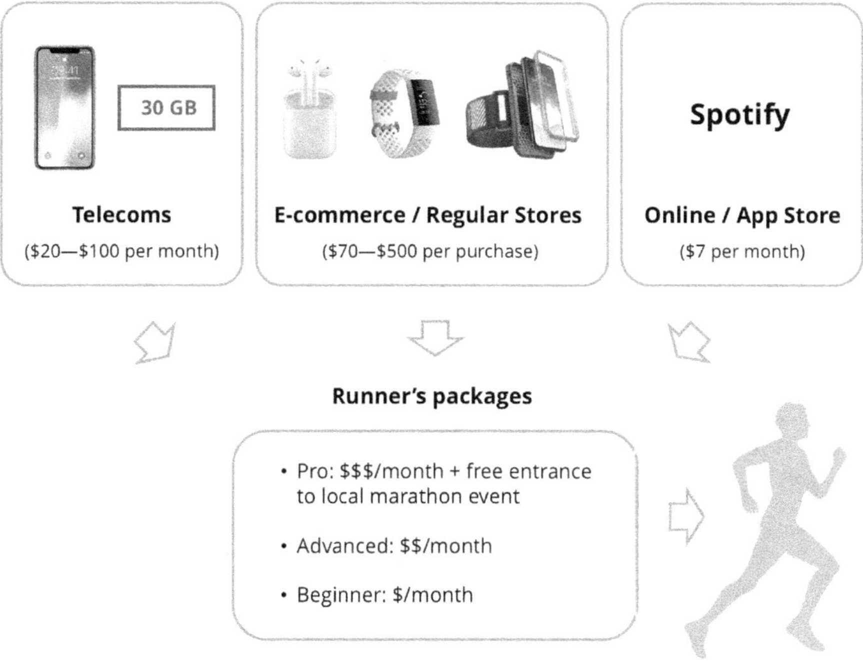

Figure 3.14: Example of a Fitness Enthusiast's Packaging Offer

- **Travelers:** Offering international roaming packages, travel insurance, language translation apps, and partnerships with travel-related services like Uber or Airbnb (see Figure 3.15)

Traveling is better with...

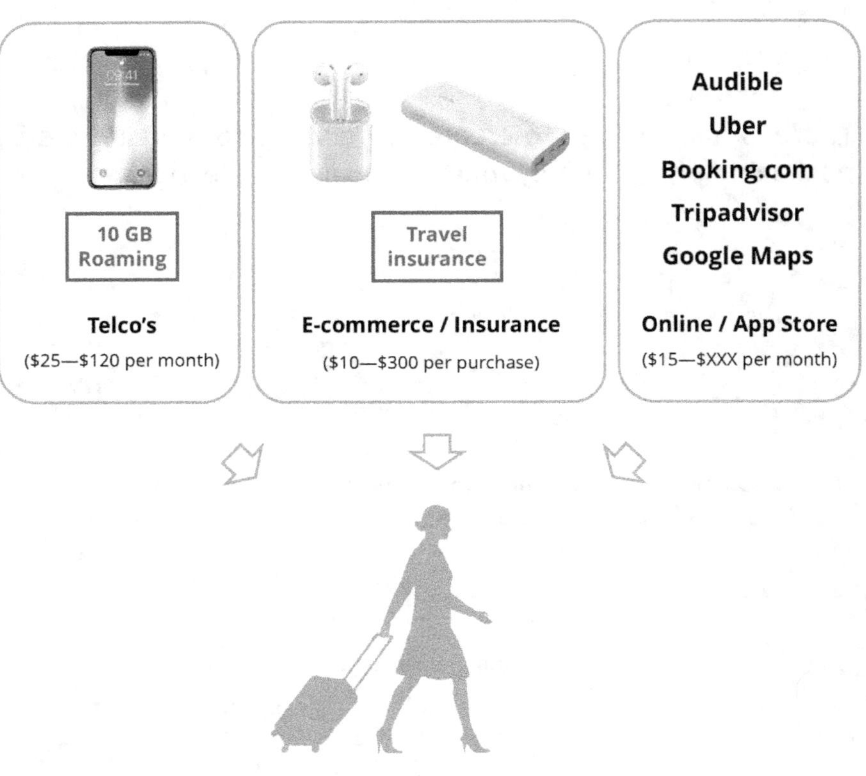

Figure 3.15: Example of a Traveler's Packaging Offer

- **Families:** Providing family mobile plans, parental control apps, educational content subscriptions, and home security solutions

- **Outdoor hobbyists:** Catering to customers like fishermen by bundling mobile devices with specialized equipment such as fish-finding gadgets (e.g., Deeper sonar devices), outdoor apps, and durable accessories

Such contextual bundles are far more compelling than generic promotions. Aligning VAS with customer needs not only drives uptake but also enriches the overall experience, improving long-term satisfaction and retention.

3.4.3.3 Capabilities

Successfully executing a VAS cross-sell program demands broad collaboration across telecom functions and external partnerships:

- **Partnerships and content:** Partnering with content providers, technology firms, and other third parties extends the range of VAS. Exclusive deals, bundled offers, and co-branded promotions give telecoms an edge in a competitive environment.

- **Billing and systems integrations:** Robust billing systems must seamlessly integrate multiple services into a single customer view. Accurate charging, unified invoicing, and easy subscription management reduce friction and encourage adoption.

- **Data analytics and lifestyle segmentation:** Advanced analytics help telecoms understand which customers might benefit most from specific VAS packages. Beyond demographic data, leveraging usage patterns and transactional histories fuels predictive models that pinpoint the right offers at the right time.

- **Channel readiness and customer service:** All inbound and outbound channels—from retail and contact centers to SMS, email, and apps—require adequate training and tools to sell and support VAS. This includes arming customer service teams with troubleshooting and escalation processes that extend beyond the telecom's own systems, ensuring that customers receive swift resolutions for third-party service issues.

From a governance perspective, the complexities of multi-party agreements, revenue-sharing models, and quality control procedures necessitate a well-defined structure for contract management, service-level agreements, and joint performance reviews. One of the most important aspects is governing the sustainability of specific VAS offerings to ensure that VAS offerings are not short-lived gimmicks but create sustained value.

3.4.3.4 Evaluation

Cross-selling VAS can deliver significant benefits, provided the right metrics and controls are in place:

- **Gains:** The uplift in ARPU, incremental revenue from VAS sales, and improvements in customer satisfaction scores or NPS. Market differentiation is another important gain, which allows you to stand out in a competitive market.

- **Costs:** Account for licensing fees, revenue-share arrangements, billing and platform upgrades, and training expenses. Evaluate channel commissions for VAS sales and ongoing operational costs, including marketing, support, and partner management.

By keeping a close eye on these areas, telecoms can validate their cross-selling initiatives and make timely adjustments to sustain growth.

3.4.3.5 Summary

VAS cross-sell strategies have evolved into an integral component of telecom growth plans. Through data-driven lifestyle segmentation and broad partnership ecosystems, you can provide customers with tailored add-ons that meet their unique preferences. This level of personalization fosters deeper engagement, boosts ARPU, and fortifies customer loyalty. However, success hinges on robust back-end systems, well-structured partnerships, and comprehensive channel readiness. Done correctly, VAS cross-sell becomes a powerful differentiator, fueling continuous value creation for both customers and the business. The CVM Canvas in Figure 3.16 provides a summary view of a VAS cross-sell program.

The Customer Value Management Canvas:
VAS Cross-sell Program

Purpose

Drive revenue growth and loyalty by offering relevant VAS that complement core telecom services

Approach

Customer Segments

- Lifestyle segments
- Behaviour segments
- Preference segments

Value Delivered

Enhance daily life by integrating convenient, personalized add-ons alongside core telecom services.

Channels

- Inbound channels (web, mobile app, point-of-sale)
- Outbound channels (email, SMS, in-app notifications)

Capabilites

Technology

- Flexible billing platform for 3rd party subscriptions
- 3rd party integrations with internal systems
- Standard CVM technology stack

Data

- Usage patterns
- Location information
- Web browsing information
- Predictive models to identify lifestyles

Collaboration

- 3rd party partnerships
- Product management
- Sales channels
- Customer service
- IT
- Data analytics

Governance

- 3rd parties contracts and revenue-sharing models governance
- Gate keeping processes to evaluate which VAS offering need to be kept over the long term

Evaluation

Gains

- ARPU increase
- Differentiated offering in a competitive market
- Stronger customer lock-in

Costs

- Licensing fees
- Revenue shares
- Billing platform upgrades
- Sales and customer service teams training
- Ongoing partner management

Figure 3.16: CVM Canvas for a Value-added Services Cross-sell Program

 ## 3.4.4 Loyalty Programs

3.4.4.1 Purpose

In the telecom industry, customers often maintain relationships with their service providers for many years. This long-term engagement presents a unique opportunity to deepen the emotional connection between the customer and the brand. Your loyalty program should aim to strengthen this bond by recognizing and rewarding customers for their continued patronage. By making customers feel valued and appreciated, you enhance their trust and commitment to your services, which becomes a crucial factor in their decision to stay with you, even when faced with competitive offers.

Customers expect acknowledgment for their loyalty. It's common to hear sentiments like, *"I've been your customer for ten years; why do you offer me the same as everyone else?"* Such feedback underscores the importance of differentiating loyal customers and providing them with exclusive benefits. A well-crafted loyalty program meets these expectations by offering personalized rewards and recognition, thereby fostering a deeper emotional connection and promoting long-term retention.

3.4.4.2 Approach

Your approach should focus on creating meaningful and personalized experiences that resonate with customers on an individual level. Strive to transform the customer relationship from a transactional interaction to an emotional connection. Key elements of this approach include:

- **Personalized rewards and recognition:** Tailor rewards to align with individual customer preferences and behaviors, demonstrating your understanding and appreciation of each customer. This could involve special offers during contract renewals, exclusive discounts on the latest devices, or invitations to premium events.

- **Simplified enrollment and onboarding:** By making it easy for customers to join and participate in the loyalty program, you enhance their initial experience and encourage ongoing engagement. A seamless onboarding process sets a positive tone for the relationship.

- **Regular and meaningful communication:** Consistent, personalized communication keeps customers informed about their rewards, program updates, and new opportunities. Timely notifications and messages reinforce their connection to the brand and maintain their interest.

- **Creating emotional touchpoints:** Identify moments in the customer journey where you can strengthen emotional bonds, such as celebrating anniversaries, acknowledging milestones, or providing support during significant life events. These gestures add a personal touch that deepens the relationship.

- **Fostering a sense of community:** Building a community among your customers enhances their connection to the brand. By offering platforms for customers to interact, share experiences, and participate in brand-related activities—such as online forums, social media groups, or exclusive events—you create a shared sense of belonging.

Understanding that customers tend to stick with their telecom provider for extended periods, you should focus on nurturing this relationship over time. By consistently delivering value and positive experiences, you cultivate loyalty that transcends mere service provision, embedding your brand into the customers' daily lives.

3.4.4.3 Capabilities

Implementing a robust loyalty program depends on well-aligned technology, operational processes, and cross-functional collaboration:

- **Loyalty platform:** In addition to the core CVM technology stack (see Section 4.3), a dedicated loyalty platform is crucial for managing points, rewards redemption, program tiers, and other specialized features. Seamless integration with billing, CRM, and analytics systems ensures a consistent experience across touchpoints.

- **Rewards program architecture:** Designing attractive and attainable rewards—ranging from partner discounts and merchandise to VIP events—requires strategic planning and vendor or partner management. A compelling rewards catalog motivates ongoing participation and helps differentiate your loyalty program.

- **Cross-functional collaboration:** Loyalty must be woven into every stage of the customer journey. Marketing, customer service, and IT teams should work together to maintain a uniform brand experience, share customer insights, and adapt the program's features as customer needs evolve. Frontline employees, in particular, play a critical role by recognizing and responding to loyalty-building moments in real time.

3.4.4.4 Evaluation

Measuring the success of loyalty programs helps validate their value and guide continual improvements. Key performance indicators include:

- **Reduced churn:** Emotionally engaged customers are more resistant to switching, which often translates into lower churn rates.

- **Improved NPS:** Customers who feel recognized and rewarded are likelier to recommend your services to friends and family, boosting your Net Promoter Score (NPS).

- **Increased CLV:** Long-standing customers with strong loyalty tend to purchase additional services and remain profitable over time, raising overall customer lifetime value (CLV).

Costs typically involve loyalty platform licenses and maintenance, rewards provisioning, and the overhead of unredeemed points (which represent future financial liabilities). By regularly evaluating both the gains—such as incremental revenue and reduced churn—and the costs, CVM professionals can ensure that loyalty programs remain aligned with strategic objectives and continue delivering a positive return on investment.

3.4.4.5 Summary

Effective loyalty programs go beyond simple point-collecting mechanisms. They cultivate deep emotional connections, acknowledge the history customers share with your brand, and make each individual feel genuinely valued. When executed well, loyalty initiatives reduce churn, enhance brand reputation, and expand the overall customer lifetime value. The CVM Canvas in Figure 3.17 provides a summary view of key aspects of a loyalty program.

The Customer Value Management Canvas:
Loyalty Program

Purpose

To deepen emotional bonds, reward customer tenure, and reduce churn through personalized recognition

Approach

Customer Segments

Long-term and engaged subscribers across prepaid, postpaid, and home services who value personalized rewards.

Value Delivered

- Meaningful rewards
- Exclusive experiences
- A sense of appreciation

Channels

- Mobile app
- Web portal
- Assisted inbound channels
- Assisted outbound channels

Capabilites

Technology

- Loyalty platform
- Integration to CVM technology stack
- Rewards catalogue

Data

- Customer usage and tenure
- Churn indicators
- Reward redemption behavior

Collaboration

- CVM
- Marketing
- IT
- Customer Service

Governance

- Processes to manage partner agreements
- Control unredeemed points liabilities
- Quarterly loyalty program performance review

Evaluation

Gains

- Reduced churn
- Higher NPS

Costs

- Loyalty platform licensing
- Rewards provisioning
- The financial overhead of unredeemed points

Figure 3.17: CVM Canvas for a Loyalty Program

3.5 Retain

The third CVM Portfolio pillar is "retain" and it groups initiatives related to making sure that the customers you want to keep do not leave you. Customer retention is key to ensuring profitable and sustainable growth. With numerous churn reasons across prepaid, postpaid, and home services, understanding and addressing the root causes of customer attrition is complex but critical. In the following sections we will define strategies that help to retain best customers in prepaid, postpaid, and home services.

 **3.5.1 Retention**

3.5.1.1 Purpose

The retention framework aims to systematically help organizations reduce churn by identifying the fundamental reasons why customers leave and addressing the issues effectively. By prioritizing targeted retention actions and continuously improving initiatives through proactive and reactive measures, you will ensure organizational alignment in delivering a superior CX that meets evolving customer needs and expectations.

3.5.1.2 Approach

No single "silver bullet" can keep customers from churning. As customers rely on more services from a single telecom, switching to a competitor becomes increasingly complex because of behavioral inertia, temporary inconvenience (e.g., installing new home services), and potential loss of bundled value.

Customers generally switch if one of three conditions arises: a major life event (moving to a new home, marriage, or a job change), significant dissatisfaction with the current service, or an exceptionally compelling competitor offer that justifies enduring the switching costs. Effective retention strategies must anticipate these triggers by focusing on customers' life changes, frustrations, and competitor actions.

Because prepaid and postpaid services have unique churn dynamics, we will analyze them separately. However, the underlying principle remains the same: identify the churn drivers, quantify their impact, and address them proactively with relevant offers and solutions.

3.5.1.2.1 Postpaid and Home Services

To retain customers, you must first understand why they churn and address those root causes. While some factors, such as service dissatisfaction or uncompetitive pricing, can be managed, other factors such as a customer's death or relocating to another country are beyond your control.

Begin by calculating churn rates by reason so that you can identify patterns and trends. Lifecycle segmentation helps you interpret churn reason data more effectively. Key lifecycle segments include (see Figure 3.18):

- **New customers** (first three months): Recently acquired customers who are in the initial phase of their relationship with you

- **On-contract customers** (from three months until contract end): Customers who are in the midst of their contractual agreement

- **End-of-contract customers** (three months before and after contract end): Customers approaching the end of their contract or recently out of contract

- **Off-contract customers** (more than three months after contract end): Long-term customers who have completed their contractual obligations

While lifecycle-based segmentation is a useful starting point, additional segmentation based on customer value, behavior, and needs can provide deeper insights to understand the type of customer churning.

Understanding the overall churn rate is essential, but identifying the specific reasons why customers leave is crucial. Analyze existing data, review exit surveys, gather customer feedback, and examine insights from customer support interactions to pinpoint these reasons within each lifecycle stage.

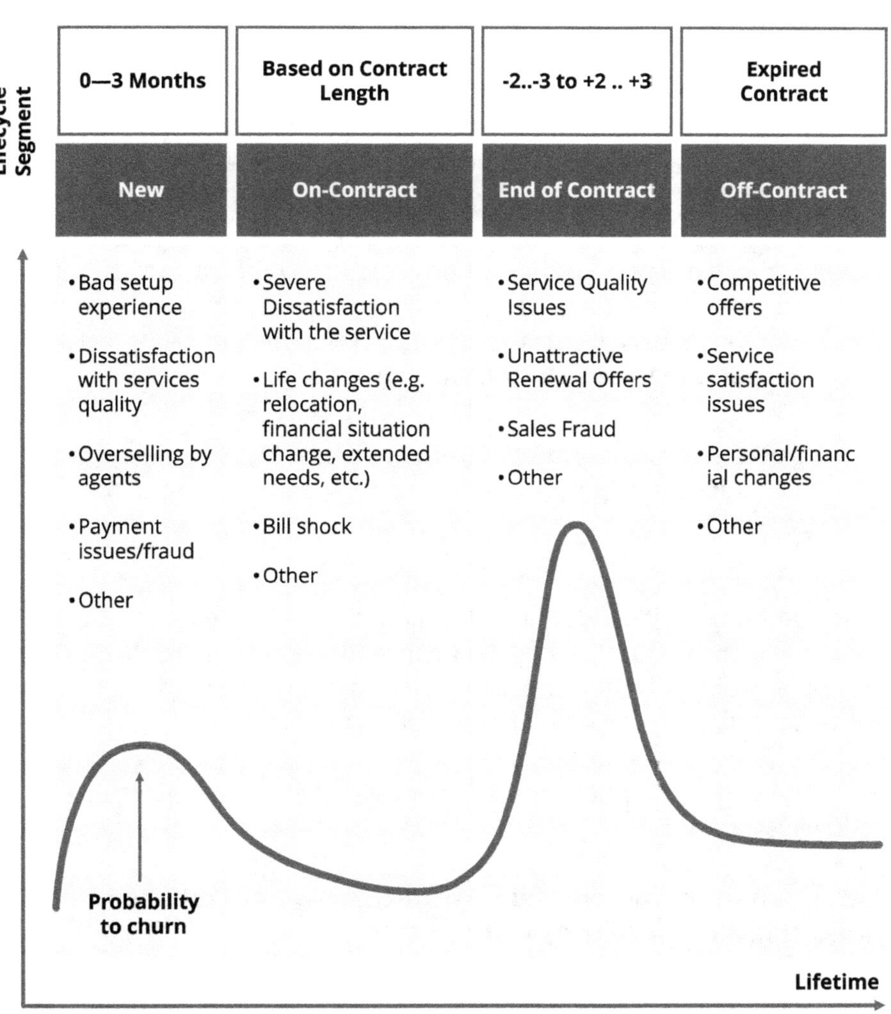

Figure 3.18: Churn Segmentation by Lifecycle

For example:

- **Initial three months:** Churn may spike due to setup experience issues, service quality concerns, payment issues, fraudulent activities, overselling by agents, and other factors.

- **On-contract period:** Churn is typically low but may occur due to severe dissatisfaction, bill shocks, or life changes such as relocation.

- **End-of-contract period:** Churn rates may increase as customers leave due to service dissatisfaction, unattractive renewal offers, or unethical sales practices like agents canceling existing contracts to issue new ones for bonuses.

- **Out-of-contract period:** Churn reasons include personal circumstance changes, competitive offers, and ongoing service dissatisfaction.

Once you have a clearer understanding of churn rates and reasons, prioritize which churn causes you can address, often creatively. For example, while you cannot prevent customers from relocating to another country, you can offer them a call-home product.

To evaluate the potential impact of addressing a churn reason, use the following formula:

Retention opportunity = Number of churners × Likelihood to address churn cause (0 to 1) × Future CLV

This calculation helps you quantify the potential benefits of multiple alternative retention initiatives, allowing you to focus on areas with the highest return.

With this clarity, you can then work to continuously identify signals that flag potential churn early and then launch appropriate retention strategies. Common churn reasons, signals, and retention initiatives are described below.

3.5.1.2.1.1 Initial Three Months

During the initial three months, setup experience or quality issues often lead to churn. Low onboarding NPS signal dissatisfaction with the setup process. To address this, you can redesign the setup process to ensure a smoother onboarding experience, enhancing customer satisfaction from the outset (view 3.3.1 Onboarding for more insights).

Service quality concerns are another common reason for early churn, indicated by negative feedback in onboarding NPS surveys. Providing proactive customer support to address service issues promptly can mitigate this concern.

Payment issues or fraud, signaled by late payments detected through billing systems, can also lead to early churn. Implementing credit checks during acquisition helps ensure that customers are financially capable of maintaining their accounts, reducing churn related to payment problems.

Overselling by agents can result in customer dissatisfaction, leading to churn. Complaints about overselling in onboarding feedback highlight this issue. Aligning sales incentives with retention objectives discourages unethical practices, ensuring that customers receive services that meet their needs without undue pressure.

3.5.1.2.1.2 On-Contract Period

During the on-contract period, severe service dissatisfaction can cause churn, although it is typically low. Low customer satisfaction scores from surveys or support interactions signal this risk. Using ML models to identify dissatisfied customers allows you to provide tailored, proactive support, addressing issues before they lead to churn.

Life changes, such as relocation, also contribute to churn during this period. Signals include customer notifications about relocation or financial difficulties. Offering flexible plans, such as temporary service suspension or downgrades, accommodates their needs and can retain the customer despite their changing circumstances.

3.5.1.2.1.3 End-of-Contract Period

At the end of the contract period, churn rates often increase. Service quality issues, signaled by declining customer satisfaction scores, can prompt customers to leave. Enhancing service delivery and addressing concerns through proactive engagement can improve retention.

Unattractive renewal offers are another reason customers may churn at this stage. Low overall renewal rates or negative feedback regarding offers highlight this issue. Utilizing NBO recommendations allows you to present compelling renewal options, encouraging customers to stay.

Sales fraud, such as unethical agents canceling existing contracts to issue new ones for bonuses, can also lead to churn. Negative NPS following sales interactions signals this problem. Realigning sales incentives to promote ethical practices and customer retention addresses this concern.

3.5.1.2.1.4 Out-of-Contract Period

In the out-of-contract period, competitive offers and ongoing service dissatisfaction are common churn reasons. Customer inquiries about cancellation or references to competitor promotions signal a risk of churn due to competitive offers. Providing personalized offers or discounts to match or exceed competitive offerings can help retain these customers.

Continued low satisfaction scores indicate service dissatisfaction. Addressing service issues directly and improving overall quality are essential to retaining customers in this segment.

Personal or financial challenges, signaled by customer communication regarding financial hardship, can also lead to churn. Offering payment plans, discounts, or service downgrades helps retain customers facing financial difficulties.

3.5.1.2.2 Prepaid

While the approach to postpaid retention begins with defining customer lifecycle stages and examining churn reasons, the prepaid service line requires a nuanced strategy due to varying market characteristics.

In some markets, prepaid price plans offer long validity periods—such as 1-month, 3-month, 6-month, or 12-month plans. In these scenarios, retention activities focus on product renewal lifecycles. Effective segmentation might include new customers, customers with more than 14 days until product expiration, customers with 14–0 days until product expiration, customers with 0–14 days after product expiration, and customers with more than 14 days after product expiration.

Conversely, in markets where pay-per-resource pricing remains dominant, prepaid segmentation revolves around customer activity levels. Segments might be defined as new customers, customers with 0–7 days of activity, 7–14 days of activity, 14–30 days of activity, 30–60 days of activity, and over 60 days of activity.

Despite these differences, the key principle remains the same: reducing churn hinges on identifying churn reasons and addressing them effectively. Apply the same principles used in postpaid retention—list all churn reasons, quantify their retention opportunities, prioritize them, identify early churn signals, and initiate targeted retention activities.

For example, during the initial three months, various factors can contribute to churn:

- **Traveling:** Travelers often purchase SIM cards at airports; their devices are first seen on the network there, are set up in foreign languages, and regularly use data services before disappearing from the network in less than 30 days. While the churn signals for travelers are highly accurate, retention actions are generally unnecessary. However, there is an opportunity to upsell and maximize customer value during their visit.

- **Fraud or misuse:** Signals include devices seen on the network with multiple SIM cards, customers disappearing a few days post-activation, and behavior flagged as fraudulent. The accuracy of these signals is high, but retention actions are not required in these cases.

- **Sales channel issues:** Indicators such as SIMs sold by agents with high churn rates, customers leaving shortly after activation, and minimal usage post-bonus period highlight this problem with high accuracy. To address this, you should align the sales channel's bonus system with retention objectives, preventing churn driven by misaligned sales incentives.

- **Rotational churn:** Devices that are associated with multiple SIM cards and customers who actively exploit acquisition offer bonuses before leaving, present another challenge. The signal accuracy is medium-to-high. Adjusting acquisition offerings to prevent abuse of bonuses or providing long-term discounts can retain these customers and reduce SIM-switching behavior.

Other churn reasons may be identified through churn prediction models, with medium-to-low signal accuracy. In these cases, deploying predictive analytics and offering personalized retention initiatives can help retain customers who might otherwise churn for unspecified reasons.

In the post three-month stage other factors can contribute to churn:

- **Infrequent users:** Some customers purchase prepaid SIM cards just to use them once in several months (e.g., when coming home to visit family from abroad). Their long inactivity flags these customers as potential churners, though this is just their regular behavior. These users can be identified by flagging SIM cards that are mostly inactive but show some irregular incoming or outgoing activity despite a positive account balance. Retention initiatives for these customers involve offering special price plans, which allows them to keep the SIM cards alive for extended periods, encouraging customers not to throw the SIM cards away.

- **Customers migrating to postpaid plans:** You can offer tailored promotions to facilitate their transition from prepaid to postpaid plans, thereby retaining them within your services.

- **CX issues:** Low NPSs, poor feedback in surveys, or negative predictions from CX models, have medium-to-low signal accuracy. To mitigate this, you should improve network quality in identified areas, provide proactive customer service, and utilize ML tools to predict and address customer dissatisfaction promptly.

- **Dual-SIM prioritization:** Customers who use dual-SIM capable devices and exhibit patterns like regular inactivity periods or selective resource usage (e.g., only data or on-net minutes) have medium signal accuracy. Retention strategies here involve employing dual-SIM identification models to create offerings that cater to mixed SIM usage patterns, encouraging customers to prioritize your services.

- **Competitive offers:** These can lead to churn, identified through churn prediction models with medium-to-low signal accuracy. By deploying these models to pinpoint at-risk customers, you can provide personalized counter-offers to retain them.

- **Device loss or theft:** This is signaled by sudden network disconnection or customer-reported lost SIMs, with medium-to-low signal accuracy. In such cases, retention actions are generally not required.

3.5.1.3 Capabilities

Retaining customers' demands coordinated, cross-functional effort. Data analytics, market research, product development, pricing, operations, customer service, and sales channels must collaborate to fix the root causes of churn.

- **Technology:** A robust CVM platform is essential for real-time detection of churn signals. Predictive analytics and ML models enable timely interventions, while campaign management tools deploy "save" offers (see Section 4.3).

- **Data:** In addition to usage and demographic data, tap into location insights, NPS scores, focus group feedback, and complaint logs to uncover churn drivers.

- **Collaboration:** Assign a dedicated cross-functional team (data analytics, market research, product development, pricing, operations, customer service, and channel teams—see Chapter 5) to design and track retention programs. Foster a shared commitment to putting customer needs first, from product managers creating valuable bundles to frontline agents offering helpful advice.

- **Governance:** Hold weekly or monthly steering meetings to review churn metrics, identify emerging trends, and prioritize retention actions. This continuous review cycle aligns all stakeholders on common goals and fosters accountability.

3.5.1.4 Evaluation

Effective retention delivers direct and measurable benefits to key commercial KPIs, however it typically takes months and sometimes years to achieve the intended retention impact:

- **Reduced churn:** Proactive detection and resolution of churn issues keep more customers in your base.

- **Increased CLV:** Targeted retention efforts for high-value customer segments boost long-term revenue.

From a cost perspective, consider program launch expenses, the cost of retention offers (e.g., steep discounts), and commission structures. Ensuring that retention investments are balanced against future revenues is vital for sustaining an attractive ROI.

3.5.1.5 Summary

A strong retention program involves identifying why your customers leave, finding early signals of dissatisfaction, and then taking decisive, customer-centric action. By combining lifecycle segmentation, advanced analytics, and proactive engagement, you can meaningfully reduce churn across prepaid, postpaid, and home services. Collaboration and transparency across multiple teams are essential in driving this effort, ensuring that the final outcome is not just lower churn but a truly loyal and satisfied customer base. The CVM Canvas in Figure 3.19 provides a summary view of key aspects of a postpaid retention program.

The Customer Value Management Canvas:
Postpaid Retention Program

Purpose

Reduce churn by systematically addressing root causes and proactively delivering solutions to meet evolving postpaid customer needs

Approach

Customer Segments

- New customers
- On-contract customers
- End-of-contract customers
- Off-contract customers

Value Delivered

- Create solutions for relevant life events (like moving house)
- Proactively address customer experience issues that cause churn
- Provide personalised retention offers for price sensitive situations

Channels

- Assisted inbound channels (point-of-sale, customers service)
- Unassisted inbound channels (self-service portal, mobile app)
- Assisted outbound channels (telemarketing)

Capabilites

Technology

- CVM platform
- Machine Learning and predictive analytics

Data

- Usage
- Demographic
- NPS
- Complaint logs
- Life-event triggers

Collaboration

- CVM
- Data analytics
- Product management
- Pricing
- Operations
- Customers service

Governance

Regular churn-metrics reviews in steering meetings, ensuring transparent alignment on retention actions

Evaluation

Gains

- Lower churn
- Higher customer lifetime value

Costs

- Program launch expenses
- Retention offer incentives
- Adjustments in sales commissions

Figure 3.19: CVM Canvas for a Postpaid Retention Program

3.5.2 Cancellations

3.5.2.1 Purpose

Cancellations can be seen as the last line of defense in retaining valuable customers. Unlike proactive retention programs that target customers before they contemplate leaving (see Section 3.5.1), cancellation programs address those who actively request to terminate their services. When inbound requests arrive, customer service professionals aim to uncover the root cause of dissatisfaction, propose relevant solutions, and highlight the benefits of staying. By meeting these customer needs promptly, cancellations can turn into opportunities that deliver immediate value and re-establish trust.

3.5.2.2 Approach

It is possible to predict which customers are more likely to churn, but it is nearly impossible to pinpoint exactly when they will contact to cancel. This unpredictability requires continuous preparedness across all assisted inbound channels (see Section 5.8). Each channel—whether call centers, retail shops, or online chat—must have clear instructions and resources to manage cancellation requests swiftly.

3.5.2.2.1 Customer Insight and Cancellation Analysis

CVM serves as the analytical backbone that prepares teams to handle cancellations effectively. Before any customer calls or walks in, CVM professionals analyze account history, usage patterns, and other relevant data. These insights allow the saves team to anticipate likely issues and have pre-approved offers ready.

For example, Emma, a postpaid customer dissatisfied with international roaming options, contacts to cancel. By analyzing her usage and complaint history, the CVM team must identify roaming as her primary concern and prepare counter offers, enabling the saves team to address it effectively.

Segmenting customers based on cancellation risk and retention potential is crucial. Jack, a long-term home services customer with high engagement, is identified as high-value. The CVM team must segment him accordingly, allowing saves agents to go the extra miles to retain this high value customer.

3.5.2.2.2 Personalized Retention Offers and Targeted Engagement

Personalization is key to turning cancellation requests into successful saves. The CVM team must design offers that directly address a customer's reason for leaving. When Jack contemplates switching due to a rival's promotional rate, the agent must be able to immediately counter with a limited-time offer (e.g., a discounted upgrade to his current plan plus a six-month loyalty bonus. Canceling customers need to recognize immediate financial benefits and the company's willingness to invest in their satisfaction.

Empathetic communication amplifies the impact of these offers. If Emma is frustrated with service disruptions, the agent should start the conversation by acknowledging her concerns and apologizing for any inconvenience. Presenting an upgraded plan or a temporary discount signals genuine intent to resolve the issue. By pairing empathy with tailored incentives, teams can address emotional dissatisfaction and financial considerations in a single interaction.

Urgency further boosts program effectiveness. Emphasizing that an exclusive offer expires soon prompts customers to weigh the immediate benefits of staying against the uncertain gains of switching. In many cases, the promise of fast and tangible relief tips the balance in the telecom's favor.

3.5.2.2.3 Swift Resolution and Retention Support

Solving the underlying problem fast often carries more weight than any promotional offer. CVM, product management, and operations teams need to empower agents to address service problems on the spot. When Emma mentions dropped calls, the agent accesses network data to confirm upgrades in her area and offers a temporary discount for the inconvenience. Immediate resolution reduces frustration and enhances retention likelihood.

Additionally, giving customers flexible retention pathways—plan adjustments, alternative billing schedules, or free service add-ons—reinforces confidence in the provider's ability to meet changing needs.

These timely reassurances reduce buyer's remorse and strengthen their relationship with the brand.

Dedicated follow-up support reinforces the retention decision. After accepting the upgraded plan, customers must receive follow-up calls to ensure their continued satisfaction.

3.5.2.3 Capabilities

A robust cancellation program relies on a solid CVM technology stack (see Section 4.3). This includes seamless integration between CVM platforms and the internal tools used by customer service and point-of-sale teams. The more customer data that agents have, the more effectively they can deliver personalized solutions.

From a cross-functional perspective, close collaboration between the CVM and customer service teams is crucial. Frontline agents must feel empowered to make on-the-spot decisions, offer customized incentives, and gather post-interaction feedback. This feedback loop informs CVM teams of emerging trends, which can lead to refined segmentation, better offers, and improved communication templates.

Governance must also include regular check-in meetings, where CVM and customer service teams review the most common cancellation reasons and track the performance of saves offers. These sessions foster a culture of continuous improvement and ensure that frontline practices stay aligned with broader CVM objectives.

3.5.2.4 Evaluation

By integrating CVM insights into saves strategies, telecoms can expect:

- **Reduced churn and higher retention rates:** Personalized solutions and empathetic communication demonstrate genuine concern for customers, creating a clear incentive to remain.

- **Increased customer satisfaction:** Proactive service recovery, flexible plans, and swift issue resolution reinforce trust in the brand.

From a cost perspective, incentives offered during saves discussions typically represent the largest expense. You need to track both the short-term costs of these incentives and the long-term benefits of retaining profitable customers. By maintaining clear metrics—such as success rates per agent, ROI on offers, and post-cancellation churn trends—CVM teams can ensure that these programs deliver optimal value.

3.5.2.5 Summary

Cancellation programs differ from proactive retention initiatives by focusing on real-time, inbound requests to terminate service. By combining thoughtful customer insights with tailored offers, empathetic communication, and swift issue resolution, customer service professionals can transform a risk of churn into a moment of renewed customer commitment. The CVM Canvas in Figure 3.20 provides a summary view of key aspects of a cancellations program.

The Customer Value Management Canvas:
Cancellations Program

Purpose

Retain valuable postpaid customers who request to cancel by addressing their core dissatisfaction and demonstrating immediate value.

Approach

Customer Segments

All postpaid customers who want to cancel their contract

Value Delivered

- Provide immediate relief from dissatisfaction
- Personalized retention incentives
- Renewed confidence in the brand's commitment

Channels

Inbound assisted channels (call centers, retail stores, and online chat)

Capabilites

Technology

CVM platform offering usage analytics, churn risk scores, and on-the-spot incentive creation for frontline agents

Data

Usage patterns, cancellation reasons, and post-interaction feedback to refine offers and measure save outcomes.

Collaboration

- CVM
- Customer service
- Product management
- Operations

Governance

Regular cross-functional reviews monitor cancellation patterns, measure success rates, and refine program guidelines

Evaluation

Gains

- Reduced number of cancellations

Costs

- Retention incentives
- Agent training

Figure 3.20: CVM Canvas for a Cancellations Program

 ### 3.5.3 Involuntary Churn and Collections

Involuntary churn occurs when customers lose access to their service due to non-payment or other billing-related issues rather than making an active decision to cancel. This differs from voluntary churn, where customers consciously end their contracts because of dissatisfaction, better competitor offers, or other personal reasons. An effective involuntary churn and collections program is integral to the retain pillar, ensuring that customers who face temporary financial challenges do not lose their connection.

3.5.3.1 Purpose

The purpose of an involuntary churn and collections program is to minimize revenue loss while preserving positive customer relationships. By detecting and supporting customers who struggle to pay on time, CVM teams not only prevent avoidable disconnections but also reinforce trust. Early engagement, guided by data-driven insights, allows you to keep essential services running and show genuine concern for customers' financial well-being.

When managed effectively, such programs contribute to a healthier customer base, boost long-term loyalty, and mitigate the negative impacts of involuntary churn. Empathetic communication and tailored payment options help customers overcome temporary hardships, proving that the service provider values their connection above mere transactions.

3.5.3.2 Approach

An involuntary churn and collections program focuses on early detection, personalized support, and empathetic communication. While standard retention programs aim to identify and address dissatisfaction or usage-related triggers, this specialized approach zeroes in on financial barriers. The program begins before customers reach the point of cancellation, thus differentiating it from cancellation-focused initiatives that intervene when someone explicitly requests to disconnect.

The approach unfolds in three phases. First, CVM teams use predictive analytics to spot at-risk customers. Next, they employ tailored messages and repayment options to ease financial burdens, ensuring that connectivity remains intact. Finally, if customers still struggle, teams step in proactively with dedicated support agents and flexible service adjustments to prevent disconnection altogether.

3.5.3.2.1 Customer Insight and Risk Assessment

Early identification of at-risk customers is essential. CVM teams analyze customer data—payment history, usage patterns, and demographic factors—to pinpoint those likely to miss payments. For example, Sophie, a postpaid customer who missed her last payment and reduced her service usage, is flagged as at risk. Recognizing this behavioral shift allows CVM teams to engage with her before the situation escalates to involuntary churn.

Predictive modeling and segmentation allow CVM professionals to prioritize high-value or long-tenured customers who require immediate attention. By targeting resources where they have the greatest impact, organizations can intervene early and prevent overdue accounts from spiraling into service disconnections.

3.5.3.2.2 Personalized Engagement and Payment Solutions

Empathetic communication is essential. Messages should acknowledge customers' circumstances without sounding punitive or threatening. For example, Sophie might receive a carefully worded email that says: *"We understand financial difficulties can happen. We're here to help you maintain your connection. Explore our flexible repayment options that can ease your situation."*

Tailored engagement strategies can include personalized messaging, self-service payment platforms, or specialized support hotlines. These options reduce friction by offering flexible terms such as installment plans, temporary fee waivers, or modified service packages that align with the customer's current budget. Establishing this sense of collaboration and support fosters trust and increases the likelihood of successful repayment.

3.5.3.2.3 Proactive Retention and Support

Beyond addressing the immediate overdue situation, the program emphasizes long-term retention. Customer service teams may offer temporary service adjustments to help customers maintain essential connectivity at a lower cost, preventing abrupt disconnections. Additionally, certain high-value or strategically important customers may benefit from incentives—such as waived late fees or bonus data allocations—once they have stabilized their payments. By remaining attentive to ongoing changes in payment behavior, customer service professionals can provide continued support and preserve valuable customer relationships. All these activities must be empowered by the CVM team.

3.5.3.3 Capabilities

Robust capabilities are required to execute involuntary churn prevention effectively.

A unified data environment underpins all decision-making. Data sources on payment patterns, usage history, credit scoring, and customer interactions must integrate seamlessly to enable accurate segmentation and predictive modeling.

Technology solutions that facilitate flexible billing and self-service portals are vital. Without the ability to customize payment plans, automate notifications, or offer digital payment channels, the entire initiative loses momentum.

Empowered frontline teams with the authority to resolve issues promptly play a crucial role. Proper training helps agents interact with empathy and adapt solutions to each customer's needs. Aligning these teams with CVM objectives ensures consistent application of policies and quick escalation for complex scenarios.

Lastly, feedback loops and governance structures ensure continuous improvement. By gathering post-interaction insights from customers like Sophie and James, the CVM team can refine communication tactics, payment plans, and support offers to align with evolving customer needs.

3.5.3.4 Evaluation

A successful involuntary churn program balances minimizing revenue loss with maintaining customer relationships. Tracking metrics such as the percentage of overdue accounts resolved before disconnection, the number of flexible payment plans adopted, and the churn rate among at-risk customers offers a clear view of the program's effectiveness.

Measuring cost efficiency is also essential. This includes quantifying capital tied up in deferred payments, technology investments for self-service platforms, and third-party collections fees. The goal is to ensure that these expenses remain aligned with the projected ROI and strategic value of retaining customers.

Ultimately, showing improvements in churn reduction, higher retention among high-value segments, and greater customer satisfaction indicates a well-executed program. Even customers who face financial challenges can become advocates if they feel supported rather than penalized.

3.5.3.5 Summary

Involuntary churn differs from voluntary cancellations in that it involves disconnections due to non-payment rather than customers consciously choosing to leave. A well-structured collections and retention program tackles financial barriers proactively, ensuring continued connectivity while addressing each customer's unique needs. The CVM Canvas in Figure 3.21 provides a summary view of key aspects of an involuntary churn and collections program.

The Customer Value Management Canvas:
Involuntary Churn and Collections

Purpose

Minimize revenue loss while maintaining positive relationships by preventing disconnections due to non-payment.

Approach

Customer Segments

Postpaid customers who exhibit payment risks or missed bills

Value Delivered

- Flexible payment options
- Empathetic support
- Preserved connectivity

Channels

Assisted inbound channels (customer service, point-of-sale)

Capabilites

Technology

- Billing systems with flexible plan management
- Machine learning capabilities

Data

- Payment history
- Usage patterns
- Credit scores
- Risk segmentation

Collaboration

- CVM
- Finance
- Customer services
- Collections
- Data analytics
- Product management and IT

Governance

Escalation processes for payment collections, policy adherence, and ongoing monitoring for continuous improvement.

Evaluation

Gains

- Reduced involuntary churn
- Higher payment recovery rates

Costs

- Technology investments into flexible billing
- 3rd party collection expenses
- Capital costs related to payment delays

Figure 3.21: CVM Canvas for an Involuntary Churn and Collections Program

3.6 Next Best Action

After reviewing the three pillars of the CVM Portfolio and key programs and initiatives within each we may easily feel overwhelmed. The customer may feel the same—there may be a lot of activities happening at once with a particular customer. However, customers should not experience CVM programs—such as onboarding, upselling, cross-selling, retention, and win-back—as separate initiatives. Instead, they should perceive a series of interactions that meet their immediate needs and adapt to their changing circumstances. You must coordinate these programs effectively through NBA approaches and contextual marketing. NBA is the key to reducing noise and focusing only on what matters most at the moment—it is called the next best action for a good reason.

3.6.1 The Importance of Customer Context

Understanding the customer's context is crucial for delivering relevant and timely interactions. Customers operate within personal circumstances that CVM professionals cannot control but must respond to appropriately. Consider the following scenarios:

- **Service disruption:** A postpaid customer experiences a home internet outage, preventing them from working remotely. Contacting them shortly after with an offer to upgrade their internet speed ignores their immediate frustration and is likely to be poorly received.

- **Financial hardship:** A customer is late on bill payments due to financial difficulties. Offering them a premium TV package and a new television set disregards their current financial strain and may damage the relationship.

- **Product availability mismatch:** An enthusiastic iPhone user is excited to receive an offer for the latest model. However, upon attempting to purchase, they discover the premium models are out of stock. This leads to disappointment and erodes trust in the brand.

- **Irrelevant advertising:** A customer browsing for new smart-phones on your website is repeatedly shown ads for 5G home devices. This misalignment between their interest and your promotions diminishes the CX.

These examples highlight the consequences of uncoordinated CVM efforts that fail to consider the customer's context. To address this, NBA approaches and contextual marketing have become essential tools for aligning our programs with customer needs.

3.6.2 Understanding Next Best Action

NBA is a strategic approach that determines the most appropriate interaction with a customer at any given moment, based on their current context and your business objectives. It goes beyond simply using ML algorithms to predict customer behavior; it requires a holistic understanding of the customer and alignment with business strategies.

3.6.3 Misconceptions About Next Best Action

A common misconception is that NBA relies solely on ML algorithms to predict the NBO by calculating the expected incremental value. This calculation often involves multiplying the conversion probability by the offer revenue for each product or service and then prioritizing offers with the highest expected value. While this method appears data-driven, it has significant flaws:

- **Overemphasis on high-revenue offers:** ML models may prioritize high-value products with low conversion probabilities over more relevant, lower-value offers. For example, the model might favor promoting a new $1,000 smartphone with a 3 percent conversion rate (yielding an expected value of $30) over a $60 annual plan upgrade with a 30 percent conversion rate (yielding an expected value of $18), even if the latter better suits the customer's needs.

- **Ignoring customer context:** ML algorithms may not account for immediate customer circumstances. A customer nearing contract expiration might receive a cross-sell offer instead of a renewal-focused interaction. Similarly, a customer who recently filed a complaint might receive promotional offers instead of service recovery actions.

- **Neglecting business priorities:** Newly launched services, like 5G home internet, may lack sufficient historical data for the ML model to recommend them, despite being strategically important for the business.

3.6.4 Implementing Next Best Action Effectively

To implement NBA successfully, you must combine customer context with business strategy, using the appropriate tools to deliver meaningful interactions.

3.6.4.1 Customer Context

- **Clear context:** When a customer's intent is explicit—for example, requesting a device recommendation in-store—you should promptly provide tailored suggestions, regardless of what your next best action is. This requires having ready recommendations for various contexts, such as device upgrades, plan modifications, or contract renewals, all at once.

- **Unclear context:** When the customer's intent is not immediately evident—such as browsing the self-service app without specific actions—you should present offers that are most relevant based on their profile, usage patterns, and behavior using NBA as a prioritizing tool.

3.6.4.2 Business Strategy

- **Hard business rules:** NBA often incorporates non-negotiable policies that must be enforced. Examples include:

  - **Policy restrictions:** Refrain from sending promotional offers to customers who are overdue on payments or have unresolved service issues.

- **Priority processes:** Focus on retention strategies for customers at high risk of churn or those nearing contract expiration. Promote newly launched services, like 5G home internet, as a priority to target segments.

- **Soft business rules:** These are flexible guidelines aimed at optimizing KPIs:

  - **KPI optimization:** Use ML algorithms to prioritize offers that improve conversion rates, ARPU, or other commercial metrics, while still respecting hard business rules.

Hard and soft business rules together combine to incorporate your business perspective.

3.6.4.3 Combining Customer Context and Business Strategy

An effective NBA solution requires integrating customer context with business strategy to determine the most appropriate action. Here's how to coordinate business rules and ML algorithms:

- **Clear customer context + hard business rules:**

  - **Example:** A customer contacts support about a billing issue. The hard business rule is to resolve the issue before any promotional activity.

  - **NBA recommendation:** Focus solely on addressing the billing concern. Do not present any offers until the issue is resolved.

- **Clear customer context + soft business rules:**

  - **Example:** A customer in-store expresses interest in upgrading their smartphone.

  - **NBA recommendation:** Provide personalized device recommendations based on their usage and preferences, potentially using ML algorithms to suggest suitable models while adhering to inventory availability and current promotions.

- **Unclear customer context + hard business rules:**

  - **Example:** A customer logs into the self-service app with no specific action taken.

  - **NBA recommendation:** Check for any hard business rule triggers, such as overdue payments or open service tickets. If any exist, prioritize communicating about these issues before making new offers.

- **Unclear customer context + soft business rules:**

  - **Example:** A customer casually browses the website without clear intent.

  - **NBA recommendation:** Use ML algorithms to present personalized offers that align with business objectives, such as promoting a new data plan to heavy data users, while ensuring that no hard business rules are violated.

As can be seen from the examples provided above, aligning NBA with contextual marketing allows you to coordinate all CVM programs effectively. By considering both the customer's immediate context and your business rules and requirements you deliver interactions that are meaningful, timely, and valuable.

3.6.4.4 Key Takeaways

- **Customer-centric focus:** Always prioritize the customer's current needs and circumstances.

- **Strategic alignment:** Balance business objectives with customer context to ensure that interactions are relevant and effective.

- **Integrated approach:** Combine hard and soft business rules with ML algorithms to create cohesive NBA recommendations.

- **Continuous adaptation:** Stay responsive to changing customer behaviors and market dynamics to maintain relevance.

3.7 Supporting the Rest of the Organization with Communication Initiatives

While CVM teams drive initiatives directly impacting customer value, they also play a crucial role in supporting other departments' needs to reach customers.

CVM teams collaborate with various department teams to facilitate communications that can significantly affect the CX:

- Working with payment collections teams, CVM teams help ensure that payment reminders are sent automatically through customers' preferred channels.

- Assisting legal and compliance teams, CVM teams help manage know your customer (KYC) processes, consent management, and compliance-related messages to ensure that they meet regulatory requirements while remaining customer-centric.

- Collaborating with network operations and IT teams, CVM teams coordinate proactive maintenance notifications and service outage alerts, keeping customers informed and minimizing frustration.

- Supporting marketing teams, CVM teams ensure that generic branding and mass market promotional messages are targeted more effectively, leveraging customer data to maximize engagement and response rates.

On the other hand, uncoordinated communication across multiple departments presents several challenges:

- Without proper coordination, customers may receive excessive or conflicting messages from different departments on the same day, leading to frustration and disengagement.

- Disparate communication efforts can result in inconsistent tone, style, or information, undermining the brand image and customer trust.

To overcome these challenges, CVM teams must:

- Implement communication governance frameworks that outline processes for message approval, prioritization, and scheduling across departments.

- Utilize centralized platforms and tools to enforce and manage customer communication policies, ensuring consistency and enabling efficient coordination.

- Create comprehensive plans that map out all customer touchpoints and messages, allowing for better timing and sequencing of communications.

- Use customer data and analytics to personalize messages, optimize send times, and monitor the effectiveness of communications across different channels.

By becoming the gatekeeper of direct-to-customer communications, CVM teams manage the volume and relevance of messages customers receive. As a result, CVM teams can effectively ensure that all interactions are meaningful and enhance the overall CX.

4. Technology and Data

4.1 Navigating Technological and Data Challenges in Customer Value Management

Today CVM teams face unprecedented technological and data complexities as well as capabilities. Integrating diverse channels, managing vast amounts of customer data, and delivering personalized experiences are now essential for acquiring, growing, and retaining customers. This chapter explores five critical technology challenges that CVM professionals must overcome to excel in their job.

4.1.1 Fragmented Channels and Touchpoints

The explosion of communication channels has fragmented customer interactions (see Figure 4.1). Traditional avenues like stores and call centers coexist with digital platforms such as mobile apps, social media, and chatbots. Assisted channels, including telesales and on-site installers, add further layers of complexity. With numerous inbound and outbound channels operating simultaneously, delivering a unified message becomes a formidable task.

According to the *CVM Trends 2025* study, over 60 percent of telecoms have fully personalized their primary channels, yet only 26 percent have achieved a true omnichannel experience. Aligning these channels to provide consistent and cohesive customer engagement remains a significant hurdle for CVM teams.

4.1.2 Integration with Legacy Systems

Many telecoms operate with a mix of legacy systems and modern technologies, making systems integration complex and time-consuming. Balancing innovation with the need to maintain stable operations requires careful strategy and execution.

The same study reports that more than 60 percent of CVM teams experience delays of months or even years when launching new communication channels, integrating with legacy systems, or adding new offers to their product portfolios. The rapid pace of digital change in-

Please indicate which communication channels are available in your organization:

	Not available	Available not personalized	Available personalized
1. SMS	0%	21.1%	68.4%
2. Email	26.3%	15.8%	52.6%
3. Mobile App	21.1%	15.8%	57.9%
4. Web self-care	26.3%	15.8%	52.6%
5. Unstructured supplementary service data (USSD)	26.3%	10.5%	57.9%
6. Interactive voice response (IVR)	21.1%	42.1%	31.6%
7. Chatbot	47.4%	26.3%	21.1%
8. Surveys	10.5%	36.8%	47.4%
9. Paper mails / Invoices	36.8%	10.5%	47.4%
10. Messengers (WhatsApp, Messenger, Viber, etc.)	31.6%	21.1%	42.1%
11. Telesales	26.3%	21.1%	42.1%
12. Customer service	5.3%	21.1%	63.2%
13. Point of sale (stores)	10.5%	21.1%	63.2%

Figure 4.1: Communications Channel Availability in Organizations

tensifies the pressure to enhance agility and scalability within telecom IT infrastructures.

4.1.3 Managing the Customer Data Explosion

The exponential growth of customer data is both an asset and a challenge. Every interaction generates data signals that, if properly harnessed, can provide deep insights into customer behavior. However, this customer data sits in many IT systems and must be extracted, cleansed, unified, and integrated into a single customer view before it becomes actionable.

Despite two-thirds of telecoms worldwide adopting state-of-the-art data warehousing and data lake technologies, only 26 percent have achieved a unified customer view (see Figure 4.2). The sheer volume and variety of data make this a daunting task for CVM teams, requiring sophisticated data management strategies.

Does your organization maintain a single, unified view of each customer across all services and interactions?

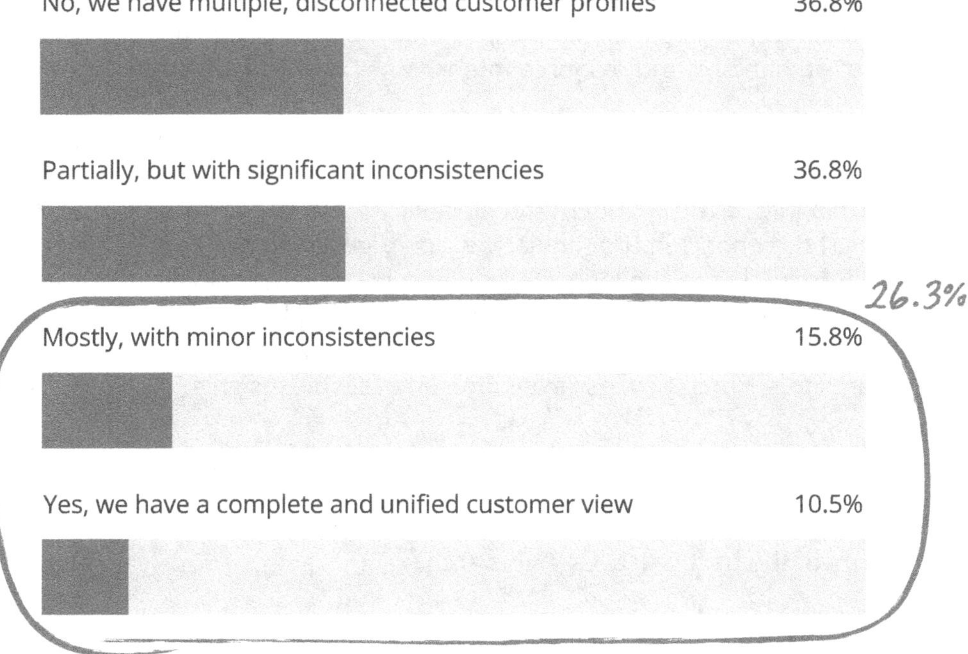

Figure 4.2: Unified View of Customer

4.1.4 Demand for Artificial Intelligence-Powered Personalization

Customers now expect personalized interactions that enhance their experience with service providers. Achieving this level of personalization necessitates extensive customer data enriched with AI, ML, and real-time decision-making capabilities.

The *CVM Trends 2025* study indicates that 53 percent of telecoms face integration times of months or years when incorporating new ML models into their CVM processes. Additionally, only 15 percent of CVM teams have implemented generative AI capabilities. These delays hinder the ability to meet customer expectations for personalized services (see Figure 4.3), even if the technological AI capabilities today are jaw dropping.

4.1.5 Complexity in Measuring Impact

In CVM, understanding which strategies truly drive results demands rigorous A/B testing, precise tracking, and comprehensive reporting. CVM processes often run simultaneously, leveraging shared logic, data, and AI/ML components with only minor differences. This interconnectedness creates significant complexity, making management both demanding and resource-intensive.

Currently, only one-third of CVM teams track their primary KPIs daily. The majority depend on weekly or monthly metrics, slowing down learning cycles and hindering their ability to accurately measure and report the impact of their initiatives (see Figure 4.4).
Addressing these challenges requires robust methodologies, such as A/B test group selection, the implementation of global control groups, advanced data modeling, and substantial effort from data engineering teams to ensure seamless execution and reliable insights.

As can be seen, five critical technology challenges require that CVM professionals carefully plan and proactively influence the technology stack that their organizations use in CVM. The next section explores some of the best practices in this area.

On average, how long does it take to implement a standard CVM activity within your organization?

	Not relevant	Days	Weeks	Months	Years	
Launch a simple batch campaign	0%	57.9%	26.3%	15.8%	0%	
Launch a simple automated campaign	5.3%	57.9%	21.1%	15.8%	0%	
Get a new campaign report	0%	52.6%	31.6%	15.8%	0%	
Extract a custom report	0%	47.4%	42.1%	10.5%	0%	
Develop new customer segments	0%	42.1%	26.3%	26.3%	5.3%	*31.6%*
Create a new audience for outbound communication	5.3%	52.6%	21.1%	21.1%	0%	
Add a new data point to the customer data set	0%	47.4%	36.8%	15.8%	0%	
Tailor product features to specific segment	0%	36.8%	42.1%	21.1%	0%	
Launch a new communication channel	0%	10.5%	26.3%	47.4%	15.8%	*63.2%*
Adjust an existing offer/price plan	0%	36.8%	47.4%	15.8%	0%	
Add a new offer/price plan	0%	26.3%	31.6%	42.1%	0%	
Automate a manual process	0%	15.8%	52.6%	26.3%	5.3%	
Deliver a new integration with internal systems	5.9%	5.9%	35.3%	47.1%	5.9%	*53%*
Create and integrate a new ML model	11.8%	5.9%	29.4%	41.2%	11.8%	*53%*

Figure 4.3: Time to Implement a CVM Activity

What KPIs does the CVM team actively track, and how frequently?

	Don't track	Ad-hoc	Monthly	Weekly	Daily
Customer base size/retention	5.3%	5.3%	36.8%	10.5%	42.1%
Churn rate	5.3%	0%	31.6%	26.3%	36.8%
Acquisition rate	5.3%	5.3%	26.3%	31.6%	31.6%
New customer acquisition cost	26.3%	21.1%	31.6%	10.5%	10.5%
On-boarding rates	10.5%	26.3%	21.1%	21.1%	21.1%
Total revenue	0%	5.3%	42.1%	15.8%	36.8%
Average revenue per user (ARPU)	0%	21.1%	47.4%	21.1%	10.5%
Customer lifetime value (CLV)	31.6%	36.8%	26.3%	5.3%	0%
Customer experience (NPS, or other)	5.3%	31.6%	47.4%	5.3%	10.5%
CVM activities incremental revenue	15.8%	26.3%	36.8%	15.8%	5.3%

Figure 4.4: Tracking CVM KPIs

4.2 Building a Future-Proof Customer Value Management Technology Stack

Constructing a CVM tech stack that delivers results quickly while creating a robust architecture as well as constantly adapting to emerging technologies is crucial. Telecoms must adhere to three fundamental architectural principles: "de-coupling" to create speed and agility for CVM teams, "modularity" by embracing flexibility and openness in architecture, and "CVM operations" to ensure scalability and resilience in critical operations.

4.2.1 De-coupling: Enabling Speed and Agility for Customer Value Management Teams

CVM teams need the ability to act swiftly without being hindered by lengthy processes caused by technological backwardness. IT departments and teams can become bottlenecks when they serve only as internal delivery units rather than strategic enablers. This often leads to CVM initiatives stalling, as requests for new integrations, essential customer data collection, or the development of communication channels get tangled in prolonged IT backlogs. In a competitive market where time-to-market is vital, such delays are unacceptable.

To overcome these obstacles, IT departments must transform into strategic partners that empower CVM teams. Providing low-code or no-code platforms allows CVM professionals to create custom parameters, workflows, and integrations independently. This approach accelerates campaign deployment and reduces reliance on IT resources.

Kamaldin Pirimbaev, Manager of Capabilities Unit, Big Data and CVM Department at Kcell AO, illustrates this shift: "Our business users can easily create custom parameters within customer profiles and utilize them in campaign design, reducing reliance on IT and accelerating time-to-market."

However, empowering CVM teams doesn't mean burdening them with complex technical tasks. It requires establishing robust technological frameworks that include clearly defined independent components, standard APIs, well documented integration protocols, automated testing, and standardized operational procedures. This ensures that, while CVM teams have the autonomy to innovate, the IT ecosystem remains manageable, secure, and stable.

4.2.2 Modularity: Embracing Flexibility and Openness in Architecture

An open and flexible architecture is essential for telecoms to adapt swiftly to new technologies and customer touchpoints. Implementing a microservices architecture breaks down the tech stack into modular, independent services. This modularity enables easier updates, the integration of new features, and simplified maintenance, supporting continuous delivery needed to respond to market changes. The trend of using mega platforms is being reversed.

Leveraging open-source technologies where they match or exceed proprietary solutions offers additional benefits. It reduces costs and enhances customization and integration capabilities. Kamaldin Pirimbaev, Manager of Capabilities Unit, Big Data and CVM Department at Kcell AO, notes: "Whenever possible, we utilize open-source solutions to maximize our budget and reinvest savings in other areas of improvement."

Open-source adoption is particularly significant in rapidly evolving fields like AI, where flexibility to switch between models is crucial due to fast-paced developments. In the context of generative AI, being able to adopt new models quickly can provide a competitive edge.

Recognizing that today's cutting-edge systems can become tomorrow's legacy, interoperability through standard integration protocols is vital. Developing universal APIs for incoming channels and establishing a central integration bus facilitates seamless communication between disparate systems. Kamaldin Pirimbaev, Manager of Capabilities Unit, Big Data and CVM Department at Kcell AO, explains their approach: "We utilize a microservices approach. For example, we have a universal API for incoming channels and a central integration bus connecting our campaign system with provisioning platforms."

This modular development strategy allows for incremental updates and reduces the time required to implement new features or integrations. It also mitigates challenges associated with legacy systems by enabling gradual replacements or upgrades with minimal operational disruptions.

4.2.3 CVM Operations: Ensuring Scalability and Resilience for Critical Operations

Since the CVM tech stack directly interacts with customers, it must be highly scalable and resilient. The proliferation of channels—from mobile apps and social media to telesales and on-site installers—demands a system capable of handling increasing loads without compromising performance.

Prioritizing cloud-based or virtualized solutions is essential. These technologies enable flexible resource allocation and provide fault tolerance, allowing the tech stack to scale with fluctuating demands and simplifying disaster recovery. Kamaldin Pirimbaev, Manager of Capabilities Unit, Big Data and CVM Department at Kcell AO, emphasizes this strategy: "We prioritize virtual servers to enable flexible resource allocation and avoid the complexities of managing dedicated hardware. This allows us to adapt quickly to changing needs and optimize costs."

Implementing well-planned, highly available components across the entire CVM stack ensures continuous operation even during system updates, outages or maintenance periods. High-availability architectures minimize single points of failure by ensuring that CVM components work even in a degraded mode, with partially available or slightly outdated recommendations and messages.

Robust monitoring and alerting mechanisms must be in place to detect and respond to failures swiftly. Considering the potential impact of issues—such as a failed ML prediction triggering incorrect campaigns—proactive measures are necessary to prevent negative CXs.

CVM operations is a new area that is rapidly developing, and many best practices are still emerging.

4.3 Customer Value Management Technology Blueprint

4.3.1 Customer Value Management Technology Reference Architecture

The CVM tech stack serves as the backbone for customer engagement, integrating multiple systems and channels. Its architecture is designed to meet the diverse technical requirements necessary for one-to-one customer communication while maintaining operational excellence.

The CVM tech stack needs to connect with various customer-facing channels such as email, SMS, mobile apps, USSD, interactive voice response (IVR), websites, chatbots, and surveys. These channels enable direct and varied interactions with customers, essential for delivering personalized experiences and enhancing engagement.

Beyond digital interfaces, it integrates with assisted channels like telesales, customer service, and point-of-sale systems. These touchpoints provide human interaction, enriching the customer experience with personalized support and fostering stronger customer relationships.

The CVM technology also aligns with telecom back-end operational systems including product catalogs, order fulfillment, and network management. This integration ensures that CVM initiatives are synchronized with telecom-specific offerings and operational workflows, allowing for seamless service delivery and operational efficiency.

Moreover, the CVM tech stack interfaces with the data and business intelligence (BI) infrastructure, supporting both batch and real-time data processing and reporting. This integration provides a foundation for data-driven insights across the organization, enabling informed decision-making and strategic planning.

Additional supporting solutions such as customer location analytics, gamification platforms, deep packet inspection (DPI) analytics, loyalty programs, consent management, and know your customer compliance systems enhance the capabilities of the CVM tech stack. These specialized systems allow for more targeted, compliant, and engaging customer interactions.

All these integrations are governed through a centralized identity and access management system. This governance ensures secure access, operational monitoring, and compliance with auditing standards, maintaining the integrity and security of CVM operations.

To meet all business and technical requirements, the CVM tech stack must include four essential components:

1. **Customer data management:** Centralizing and managing customer data to create a unified customer view

2. **Campaign management and real-time decisioning:** Orchestrating customer interactions and making instant decisions based on customer behavior

3. **AI/ML capabilities:** Leveraging AI and ML to personalize experiences and predict customer needs

4. **Measurement and reporting:** Providing analytics and reporting to measure performance and guide strategies

In the following sections, we will delve into each of these components, exploring their roles and contributions to effective customer value management in the telecom sector.

4.3.2 Customer Data Management

"First of all, it's really important to know what's important for the different customers. And you can't do that if you don't know your customers and the customer data and the customer profile. That's when you can start to map different customer groups and figure out how they act and what's important to them. To be able to catch their attention, we need to know more about our customers. So I guess that's why it's important, because when we are starting to work on the communication, it always starts with the data and the customer profile. So that's more or less the beginning in many cases to customer communication. If you don't have that in place, it's hard to get started."

— Sanna Emtinger, Head of CVM & MarTech at Telia Norway

Telecoms handle an enormous volume of customer data generated from internal sources. With tens or even hundreds of systems contributing to customer understanding, the data landscape is vast and intricate. This complexity arises not only from the sheer amount of data but also from the multifaceted customer relationships inherent in the telecom industry. Customers may have multiple subscriptions, belong to households, share joint services, or represent entire organizations in B2B accounts. Navigating this web of relationships presents significant challenges in creating a unified and actionable view of the customer.

Despite more than half of telecoms reporting advanced capabilities in data warehousing and customer data management, only 26 percent of CVM teams have achieved a truly unified customer view. This gap highlights the difficulty in integrating diverse data sources and hierarchies to deliver cohesive and personalized experiences. Without a single customer view, tailoring interactions effectively becomes a challenge, leading to missed opportunities in enhancing customer engagement and loyalty.

4.3.2.1 Understanding Data Complexity in Telecoms

The customer data collected by a typical telecom spans various categories:

- **Products and price plans:** Details of subscribed services, bundled offers, and pricing structures

- **Demographic information:** Age, gender, location, and other personal attributes

- **Consumption patterns:**

  - **Mobile usage:** Voice calls, SMS, data consumption metrics
  - **Broadband and TV usage:** Streaming habits, channel preferences, peak usage times
  - **Customer interactions:**
  - **Customer service engagements:** Reasons for contacting support, issue resolutions, feedback from call centers and

in-store visits

- **Digital touchpoints:** Website and app usage statistics, click-stream data

- **Behavioral data:**

  - **Location information:** Movement patterns, frequently visited areas

  - **Browsing history:** Web and app browsing activities, insights from DPI analytics

  - **Device information:** Types of devices used, operating systems, device capabilities

- **Engagement data:**

  - **Campaign interactions:** Responses to marketing campaigns, open rates, click-through rates

  - **Social media activity:** Engagements on social platforms, sentiment analysis

- **Financial transactions:** Payment histories, account balances, recharge patterns for prepaid customers

- **Third-party data:** Information from cookies, partnerships, and external databases

Each data point adds depth to the customer profile but also increases the complexity of data integration and management. For example, a customer might use multiple devices, have several service subscriptions, and interact with various channels, both digital and physical. Capturing and unifying this data requires robust systems capable of handling high volumes and velocities of information.

The modern CVM tech stack recognizes this and places customer data at the center of the architecture, in a dedicated platform – the customer data platform.

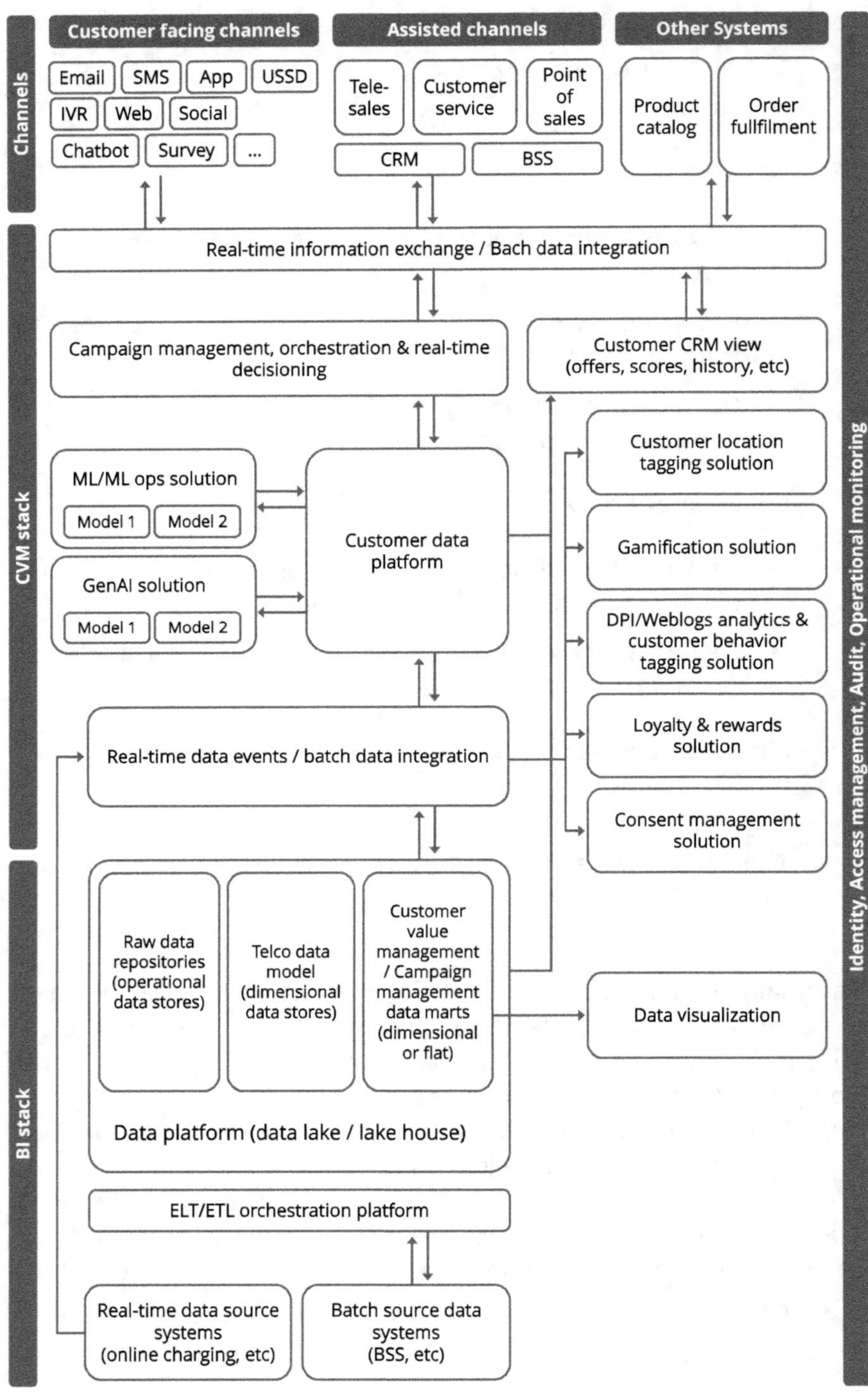

Figure 4.5: Customer Data Platform

4.3.2.2 The Role of the Customer Data Platform

To manage this complexity, telecoms employ customer data platforms (see Figure 4.5). A customer data platform (CDP) serves as the central repository for all customer information necessary for CVM functions. It integrates seamlessly with key systems like campaign management tools, AI/ML models, and business process applications, enabling telecoms to deliver personalized and timely CXs.

The CDP empowers CVM teams by providing fast and easy access to comprehensive customer profiles as well as giving them a self-service capability to do modifications like adding and deriving new customer attributes. This accessibility allows CVM professionals to independently analyze data, design targeted campaigns, respond swiftly to market shifts, and enhance customer engagement without putting extra work on busy BI teams.

4.3.2.3 Customer Data Platform vs. Data Lake and Data Warehouse

Understanding the distinction between a CDP, a data lake, and a data warehouse is crucial for effective data management.

- **Customer data platform:** A CDP is a system that collects and unifies customer data from multiple sources to create a single, comprehensive customer profile for CVM use. The CDP is specifically designed for CVM, marketing and CX purposes, enabling real-time personalization and engagement across channels.

- **Data lake:** This is a storage repository that holds vast amounts of raw data in its native format. It can include structured, semi-structured, and unstructured data. Data lakes are ideal for storing large volumes of data that may or may not be immediately useful but could be valuable for future analysis. It is a multi-purpose tool that is quite low level and technical in nature.

- **Data warehouse:** This is a centralized repository that stores processed and structured data, optimized for query and analysis. It is designed to support BI activities, providing historical insights based on data from various sources. It is a tool that is designed mainly for reporting purposes.

In the telecom context, data lakes and data warehouses handle the heavy lifting of cleansing and aggregating large volumes of data, such as call detail records (CDRs), location analytics, and DPI data. They process and store this data, making it available for various organizational needs.

The CDP, on the other hand, focuses on customer-centric data relevant to CVM activities. It ingests the processed data from the data lake and data warehouse, along with real-time data streams and low-volume events. The CDP then unifies this information to create actionable customer profiles that drive personalized marketing and engagement efforts.

By recognizing and clarifying separate functions of data lakes, CDPs and data warehouses telecoms optimize their data architecture. The data lake and data warehouse serve as the foundational layers for data storage and processing, while the CDP leverages this processed data to empower CVM teams to leverage customer data easily and in a self-service way.

4.3.2.4 Core Functions of the Customer Data Platform

The CDP performs several key functions:

- **Data ingestion and integration:** It loads data from data lakes and, if needed, directly from billing systems, CRM platforms, network data sources, and third-party providers, supporting both batch and real-time data updates. For example, integrating real-time location data enables location-based marketing campaigns, such as sending offers when a customer is near a retail store.

- **Data cleansing and normalization:** CDP needs to carry out basic data cleansing and standardization, maintaining high data quality and consistency when loading various data sources. This is critical when combining data from different systems, such as aligning customer identifiers across mobile and broadband services.

- **Unified customer profiles:** It builds consolidated profiles that include behavior, transaction history, preferences, and interactions across all touchpoints. Merging in-store purchase history with online browsing behavior can reveal cross-selling opportunities, etc.

- **Customer hierarchy management:** It manages multi-level customer hierarchies, linking individual subscriptions to a single customer and grouping customers into households or corporate accounts, and mapping all of this to digital channels, campaigns, and interactions. This is even more vital in B2B contexts, where services are managed at an organizational level but used by individual employees.

- **Real-time data processing:** It updates customer information in real time to support immediate decisions and personalization. For example, if a customer reaches their data limit, the CDP may be part of the IT chain that instantly triggers a notification with options to purchase additional data.

- **Advanced segmentation and analytics:** It provides tools for dynamic segmentation, allowing CVM teams to create highly targeted customer groups based on attributes and behaviors. For example, it can identify customers with high ARPU who are heavy data users and have recently experienced service issues for a retention campaign.

- **Integration with AI/ML models:** It incorporates outputs from ML models, such as churn predictions or propensity scores, directly into customer profiles. This integration enables more precise targeting and AI-driven personalization in campaigns.

- **Data accessibility and governance:** Secure APIs and access controls ensure that only authorized personnel can access sensitive customer data, maintaining compliance with regulations like EU GDPR. Data governance policies enforce data quality and usage standards.

- **Scalability and performance:** It is designed to handle high volumes of data and transactions, ensuring consistent performance as the business grows.

4.3.2.5 Integration with Campaign Management and Telecom Systems

The CDP serves as the foundation for the CVM tech stack that relies on customer data, including:

- **Campaign management systems (CMS):** By providing real-time data, customer segments, and predictive scores, the CDP enables precise and personalized communications across channels like SMS, email, mobile apps, and social media. For example, if the CDP shows that a customer frequently engages with the mobile app but rarely opens emails, the CMS can prioritize in-app notifications for that individual.

- **Assisted channels:** Customer service representatives and in-store personnel may view enriched customer profiles to enhance interactions. When a customer contacts support, the agent can see recent issues, service usage patterns, and potential upsell opportunities, leading to more effective and personalized service.

These integrations ensure that all customer-facing systems operate with accurate and consistent data, promoting a cohesive and personalized CX across all touchpoints.

4.3.2.6 Ownership and Governance

Typically, the CVM team owns the CDP, underscoring their strategic importance in managing customer value. This ownership model allows the CVM team to prioritize enhancements that align with business goals and customer needs. However, strong governance is essential to maintain data quality, security, and compliance with regulatory requirements.

Collaboration with IT, BI, and data governance teams is crucial. IT provides the infrastructure and technical support, BI ensures data accuracy and analytics capabilities, and data governance oversees policies and compliance. Together, they establish protocols for data access, implement security measures to protect sensitive information, and ensure that data usage adheres to legal and ethical standards.

For example, implementing role-based access controls prevents unauthorized access to personal customer data, while audit logs track data usage for accountability. Regular data quality checks and validation processes ensure that the information within the CDP remains reliable and valuable for decision-making.

By placing CDP at the core of the technology stack, telecoms make sure that the architecture is built on a solid ground for the next generation. It is a sizeable undertaking, but well worth it, considering its central future role.

"The implementation part can take, I think, between two to four years. Something like that. It took a lot of time. And sometimes, sometimes you cannot even phase out the legacy system. But this is, okay, now I'm talking about a complex organization. So we had hundreds of campaigns running, and you need to migrate everything. And then you also have a period where tooling is running beside each other. So you have your legacy system and your new system. And when do you actually switch it off? You also need to compare the outcomes of the new system with the old system to make sure everything is migrated correctly."

— Kwame van Eijndhoven, Owner of Kwadata

4.3.3 Campaign Management and Real-Time Decisioning

The campaign management and real-time decisioning systems are vital components of the CVM tech stack that enable telecoms to orchestrate interactions across all customer channels effectively.

4.3.3.1 Empowering Customer Value Management Teams with Low-Code Integration

To stay competitive, CVM teams must rapidly design and deploy marketing campaigns without being slowed down by lengthy IT development processes. Modern campaign management platforms offer low-code or no-code capabilities, allowing CVM professionals to quickly integrate new channels and create campaigns independently. This agility empowers the CVM team to respond swiftly to market changes and customer needs.

For example, if a telecom wants to launch a new prepaid data bundle targeting young adults who are heavy social media users, the CVM team can use the platform to segment the target audience, design the campaign, and deploy it across relevant channels like SMS, mobile app notifications, and social media ads—all without IT intervention, and all in a day.

4.3.3.2 Core Functions of the Campaign Management Platform

The campaign management platform serves as the central hub for managing all marketing activities. Its key functions include:

- **Omnichannel integration:** It seamlessly connects with various customer-facing channels such as email, SMS, mobile apps, websites, social media platforms, call centers, and retail outlets. This ensures consistent messaging and a unified CX across all touchpoints.

- **Campaign orchestration:** It provides tools to create and manage complex campaign workflows, schedule communications, and automate interactions based on customer behaviors and preferences.

- **Segmentation and targeting:** It enables CVM teams to access customer segmentation data from the customer data platform, such as demographics, usage patterns, and engagement history, allowing for precise targeting.

- **Personalization:** It utilizes customer data and insights from AI/ML models to tailor content and offers to individual customers, enhancing relevance and engagement.

- **Analytics and reporting:** It offers real-time monitoring and analytics to measure campaign performance, facilitating continuous optimization and informed decision-making.

4.3.3.3 Enhancing Engagement with Real-Time Decisioning

Real-time decisioning adds another layer of sophistication by enabling immediate, contextually relevant interactions. It processes real-time customer data to determine the best action at the moment of engagement.

Key features of the real-time decisioning system includes:

- **Event processing:** It handles real-time events and triggers, such as a customer browsing specific services on the website or reaching their data limit, enabling immediate responses.

- **Decision engine:** It applies business rules and AI/ML insights to decide on the NBA, offer, or message for each customer in real time.

- **Feedback loop:** It continuously captures customer responses to refine decision-making algorithms and improve future interactions.

For example, if a postpaid customer frequently exceeds their data allowance, the real-time decisioning system can immediately offer a data top-up or an upgrade to a higher-tier plan via a mobile app notification or SMS, increasing the likelihood of acceptance and enhancing customer satisfaction.

4.3.3.4 Integration with the Rest of the Technology Stack

The campaign management and real-time decisioning systems are deeply integrated with other components of the CVM tech stack:

- **Customer data platforms:** They rely on the CDP for up-to-date customer profiles, preferences, and interaction history, which inform targeting and personalization strategies.

- **AI/ML models:** They leverage predictive analytics and recommendations to enhance decision-making processes and personalize customer engagements.

- **Generative AI solutions:** They integrate with generative AI to create dynamic and personalized content, such as customized offers or messages.

- **Channel integration layers:** They ensure seamless delivery and receipt of communications across all customer-facing and assisted channels.

- **Operations and business support systems:** They interact with operational systems like order fulfillment and customer service platforms to trigger or respond to workflows that enhance the CX.

4.3.3.5 Collaborative Ownership and Governance

Typically, the CVM team owns the campaign management and real-time decisioning systems, allowing them to drive customer engagement strategies effectively. Close collaboration with IT is essential to ensure governance, security, and compliance. By providing low-code platforms and standardized APIs, IT enables the CVM team to innovate rapidly while maintaining control over the technology environment.

4.3.4 AI and Machine Learning Capabilities

Personalization in telecoms hinges on AI and ML algorithms, but implementing these algorithms often presents significant challenges. Telecoms grapple with integrating vast amounts of customer data, deploying complex models, and maintaining them over time. The sheer volume and diversity of telecom data, coupled with the need to deliver personalized experiences at scale, make this a daunting task.

According to the CVM Trends 2025 study, 53 percent of telecoms require months or even years to integrate new ML models into their CVM processes. This delay hampers their ability to respond swiftly to market changes and evolving customer needs, diminishing competitiveness and customer satisfaction. This is a far cry from the agility reported by startups and digital-first companies and is a major potential area for improvement in the future.

4.3.4.1 The Role of Machine Learning Operations in Streamlining Machine Learning Implementation

Machine learning operations (MLOps) addresses these challenges by providing the infrastructure and workflows necessary to manage the entire lifecycle of ML models. MLOps is essential for tasks like churn prediction, credit scoring, device upgrade recommendations, and strategies for migrating prepaid customers to postpaid plans. By standardizing how models are developed, deployed, and monitored, MLOps reduces time to deployment and enhances model reliability, ensuring that ML initiatives align efficiently with business objectives.

"We see that initially it took a lot of time to build the first model, but now iterations are a lot quicker because we have deployed an MLOps environment with templates. You have data, you just put everything quickly. Maybe you just add some additional data. So playing in that sandbox environment gets a lot quicker with the MLOps platform."

— Justas Jankūnas, AI/ML Area Lead at Exacaster

"That is the moment when you start to somehow design machine learning ops or machine learning operations. You need to have an automated way to track the model calculations, quality of the data, and quality of the model output. You need to have all this automated. Judging by our experience, preferably on the cloud, because having many models on-premise for us, pretty early or pretty low on the number of models, we had data scientists queuing on the weekend to recalculate the model—some horror stories. After cloud migration, suddenly it was all easy. So somehow you need to migrate the data and the models to the cloud."

— Marek Wiktor Grabowski, B2C Customer Value Management Director at Orange Poland

4.3.4.2 Enhancing Personalization and Decision-Making

Operationalizing ML models through MLOps significantly boosts personalization capabilities. CVM teams can predict numerous aspects of customer behavior, enabling instant personalization in offers and communications. Continuous monitoring and retraining of models improve predictive accuracy, leading to more effective targeted campaigns and engagement strategies.

Integrating MLOps with decisioning systems further enhances this capability. Automated, data-driven decisions become possible, empowering CVM teams to craft impactful campaigns that elevate customer value. For example, if a model predicts a high likelihood of churn for a particular customer, the decisioning system can automatically trigger a retention offer.

4.3.4.3 Understanding the Technical Components of Machine Learning Operations

To appreciate the benefits of MLOps, it's important for CVM professionals to understand its key technical components:

- **Data integration tools:** These tools help to prepare data for ML tasks.

- **Model development environments:** Platforms like Jupyter Notebooks allow data scientists to experiment with algorithms and develop models using libraries like Pandas for data manipulation, Scikit-Learn for traditional ML algorithms, and TensorFlow or PyTorch for deep learning.

- **Version control systems:** Tools like Git track changes to code and models, ensuring that developments are documented and can be reproduced. This is crucial for collaboration and compliance.

- **Containerization technologies:** Docker and Kubernetes package models and their dependencies into isolated environments called containers. This makes deployment more consistent and scalable across different systems.

- **Continuous integration/continuous deployment pipelines:** These pipelines automate the testing and deployment of models, reducing manual errors and speeding up the rollout process.

- **Monitoring and logging tools:** Solutions like Prometheus and Grafana provide real-time insights into model performance and system health, allowing for proactive issue resolution.

As telecoms scale their ML efforts, they may deploy hundreds of models to address different CVM needs. Managing this complexity requires robust automation and standardization. Automated deployment pipelines ensure that models are consistently updated without manual intervention. Continuous monitoring helps detect performance degradation, allowing for timely retraining or adjustment.

Effective version control ensures reproducibility and compliance, which is essential when models impact customer interactions. Containerization technologies help manage different model versions and allocate computational resources efficiently. Implementing failover mechanisms and redundancy strategies mitigates risks associated with model failures, maintaining operational stability and customer satisfaction.

4.3.4.4 Embracing Open-Source Tools for Flexibility

Building an MLOps solution with open-source tools aligns with the principles of flexibility and adaptability. Open-source technologies provide access to the latest advancements without vendor lock-in, allowing telecoms to customize solutions to their specific needs. Open standards ensure compatibility with other systems like CDPs and campaign management tools, enhancing interoperability and reducing costs.

By leveraging tools such as TensorFlow for model development, Kubeflow for orchestration, and MLflow for tracking experiments, telecoms can establish an adaptable MLOps framework. These tools integrate smoothly with existing infrastructure, supporting scalable and maintainable ML pipelines that evolve with technological advancements.

4.3.4.5 Ensuring Reliability and Building Trust

With numerous ML models in production, reliability is paramount. Automated testing and real-time monitoring detect issues early, ensuring that models perform as expected. Fallback mechanisms maintain service continuity in case of failures. Adhering to MLOps best practices ensures that models are robust, secure, and compliant with regulations, upholding customer trust.

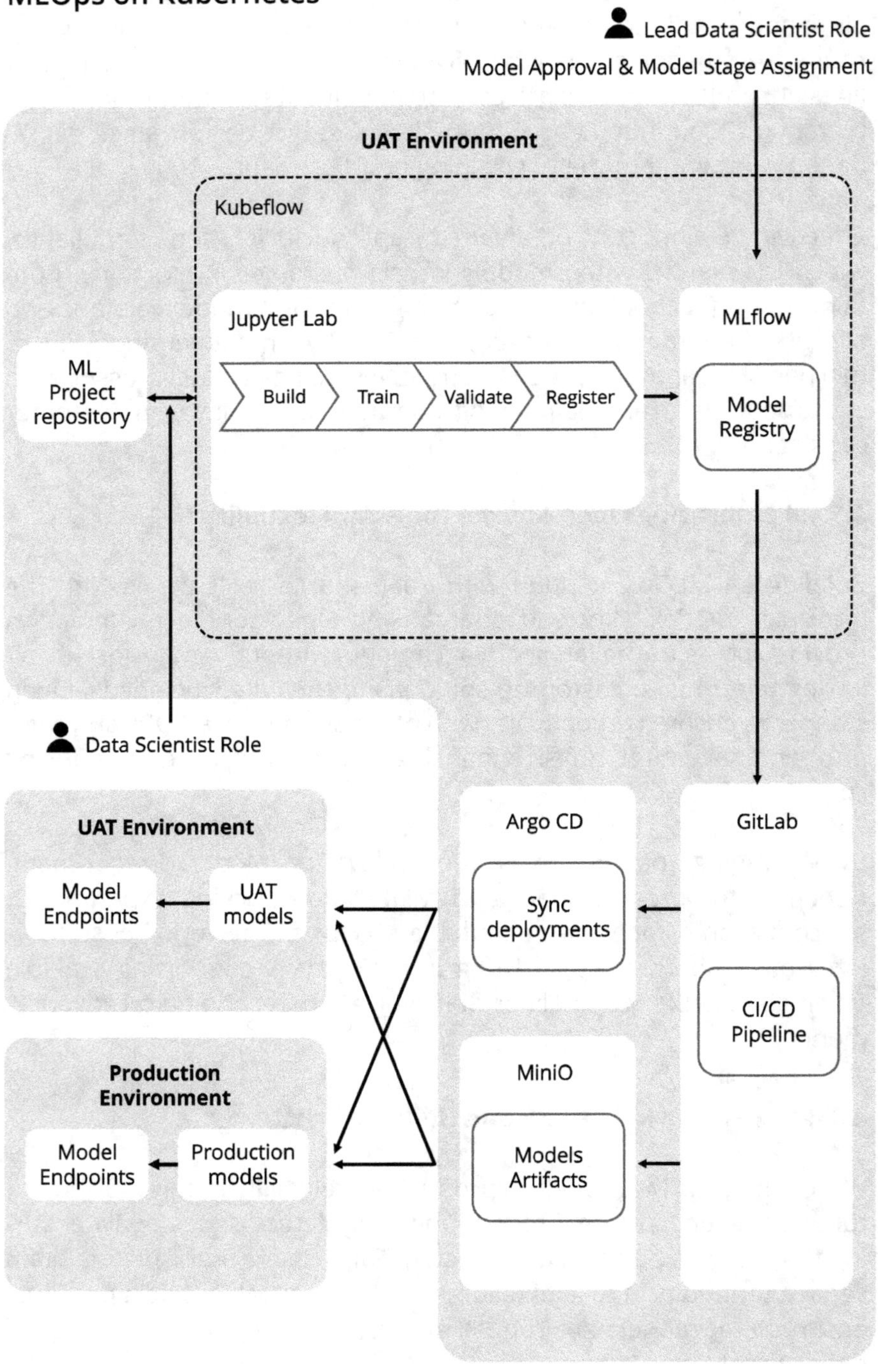

MLOps on Kubernetes

Figure 4.6: An Example of an MLOps Framework on Kubernetes

For CVM professionals, this reliability translates to consistent customer experiences and effective campaigns. Understanding the safeguards in place allows them to confidently leverage ML models in their strategies.

4.3.5 Automated Reporting Capabilities

CVM professionals strive to enhance customer engagement, reduce churn, and optimize CLV, but demonstrating these contributions can be challenging. The CVM data mart emerges as a critical enabler, with automated reporting capabilities that provide clear insights into the effectiveness of CVM strategies.

4.3.5.1 Understanding the Importance of the Customer Value Management Data Mart

The CVM data mart is a specialized extension of the BI environment tailored for CVM needs. It serves as a centralized repository that collects, processes, and analyzes data related to CVM activities. By aggregating information from multiple sources, the data mart allows CVM professionals to assess campaign performance, understand customer behaviors, and measure the overall impact on key business metrics like ARPU and churn rates.

4.3.5.2 Building a Robust Impact Measurement Methodology

Developing an effective reporting framework involves several critical steps aimed at ensuring that CVM activities can be accurately tracked and analyzed:

- **Implementing global control groups:** Establishing control groups is essential for unbiased measurement of campaign effectiveness. By comparing outcomes between customers exposed to CVM initiatives and those who are not, CVM teams can isolate the true impact of their strategies.

- **Designing target and control group selection methodologies:** Tailoring control groups to specific campaigns enhances the precision of impact analysis. This involves defining criteria for customer inclusion, ensuring statistical significance, and accounting for external variables that may influence results.

- **Standardizing campaign practices:** Consistency in campaign configuration is vital for reliable data analysis. This includes, for example:

    - **Campaign naming conventions:** Developing a systematic approach to naming campaigns aids in data organization and retrieval.

    - **Offer naming conventions:** Standardizing offer names ensures clarity when analyzing which promotions drive results.

4.3.5.3 Designing the Customer Value Management Data Mart Architecture

The architecture of the CVM data mart must align with the analytical needs of CVM professionals while integrating seamlessly with existing BI systems. Key components include:

- **CVM Portfolio and CVM program metadata:** Metadata related to the CVM Portfolio, CVM programs, initiative start and end dates, investments made, etc.

- **Campaigns domain:** Structured data related to campaign execution, such as timing, channels used, target audiences, offers delivered, offer accepted, etc.

- **NBA, NBO, ML domain:** Structured data related to intermediate calculations of NBA, NBO, ML model versions and outputs, etc.

- **Offers domain:** Captures details about specific offers, including offers prices, discount sizes, etc.

- **Customer domain import:** Links campaign and offer data to customer data from traditional BI data warehouse thus enabling comprehensive analysis of responses and behaviors

This structured approach facilitates in-depth reporting and supports advanced analytics, helping CVM professionals make data-driven decisions.

4.3.5.4 Delivering Comprehensive and Automated Reporting

Effective reporting focuses on metrics directly related to CVM objectives. Critical metrics include:

- **ARPU:** Measuring additional revenue generated per user due to CVM initiatives.

- **Churn score:** Assessing reductions in customer churn rates attributable to campaigns.

- **CLV:** Evaluating how CVM efforts enhance the long-term value of customers.

- **Customers retained or acquired:** Tracking the number of customers saved from churning or gained through CVM activities.

- **ROI:** Calculating the financial return of campaigns relative to their costs.

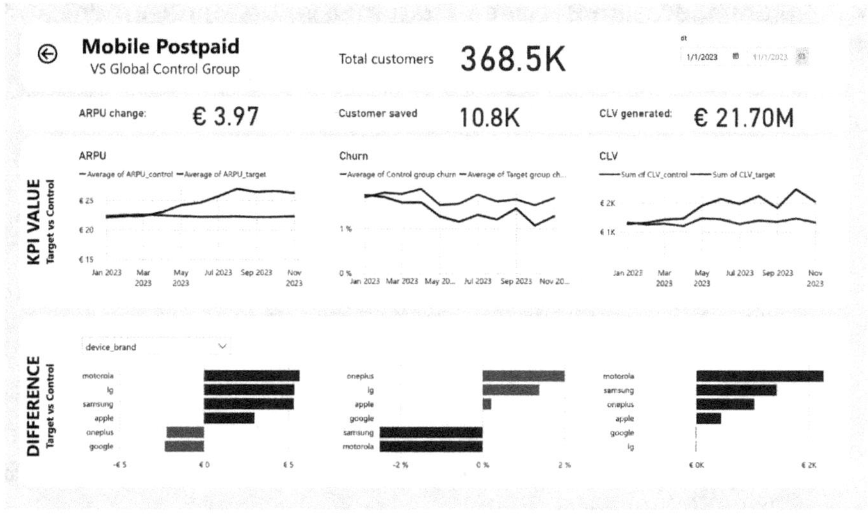

Figure 4.7: ARPU, Churn, and CLV Reporting Examples

4.3.5.5 Tracking Technical and Operational Metrics

In addition to financial metrics, monitoring technical and operational aspects provides deeper insights:

- **Campaign-level data:** Information about overall campaign execution and reach

- **Message-level data:** Analysis of individual communications sent to customers

- **Channel performance:** Evaluating the effectiveness of different communication channels like SMS, email, and app notifications

- **Timing analysis:** Understanding how the time of day, week, or year affects campaign outcomes

- **Recommendation strategies:** Assessing the impact of different recommendation algorithms or personalization tactics

4.3.5.6 Collaboration Between Customer Value Management and Business Intelligence Teams

While CVM teams drive the need for impact measurement, the development and maintenance of the CVM data mart are typically the responsibility of the BI team. This collaboration ensures that:

- **Technical expertise is leveraged:** BI specialists bring necessary skills in data warehousing, extract, transform, load (ETL) development, and reporting tools.

- **Consistency across the organization:** Utilizing the BI infrastructure promotes standardization in data handling and reporting methodologies.

- **Efficiency in resource utilization:** Centralizing data management within the BI team avoids duplication of efforts and optimizes resources.

The CVM data mart is an indispensable component in quantifying the success of CVM initiatives. By establishing a robust methodology for impact tracking and collaborating closely with the BI team, CVM professionals can effectively demonstrate their contributions to key business objectives. This not only validates the value of CVM strategies but also informs future initiatives, driving continuous improvement in customer engagement and profitability.

4.3.6 Navigating the Path to an Optimal Customer Value Management Technology Stack

Most organizations already have some or even all elements of the described CVM architecture in place. Some components function well, while others may be outdated or need replacement. Understanding the complete CVM reference architecture provides a roadmap for enhancing these existing systems without requiring a total overhaul.

By clearly defining the roles of each module and promoting modularity, you can align your architecture with a strategic architectural vision. This approach helps you identify missing pieces or underperforming components and plan targeted transformations toward your ideal setup. Achieving the perfect CVM tech stack is a journey that takes time and demands strong technical leadership—and it never ends.

Technical leadership is crucial in maintaining the integrity of a microservice-oriented architecture. With numerous solutions available in the market, it's easy to introduce redundant capabilities. For example, embedding a generative AI model within an email platform might seem beneficial initially. However, challenges arise when the same model is needed for chatbots or when customer segmentation data becomes inaccessible to other channels because it's confined within a specific system.

For telecom CVM professionals, maintaining architectural discipline ensures that each capability is implemented in the right place. This strategic focus enhances the agility and flexibility of the CVM tech stack, enabling you to adapt more effectively over time. While having multiple choices is advantageous, a disciplined approach prevents fragmentation and promotes seamless integration across systems.

In conclusion, achieving the ideal CVM tech stack is not an overnight task. It requires a clear vision, strategic planning, and the dedication to guide your organization through incremental improvements. As telecom CVM professionals, embracing this journey not only enhances your technical capabilities but also positions you to drive meaningful customer value and stay ahead in the competitive telecom landscape.

5. Cross-functional Collaboration

CVM thrives on cross-functional collaboration. Without seamless integration across functions, delivering exceptional CXs becomes an impossible challenge.

As Kristine Raumane, Head of Customer Value at Tele2 Latvia, puts it:

"Our customer base management team is all about connecting different departments."

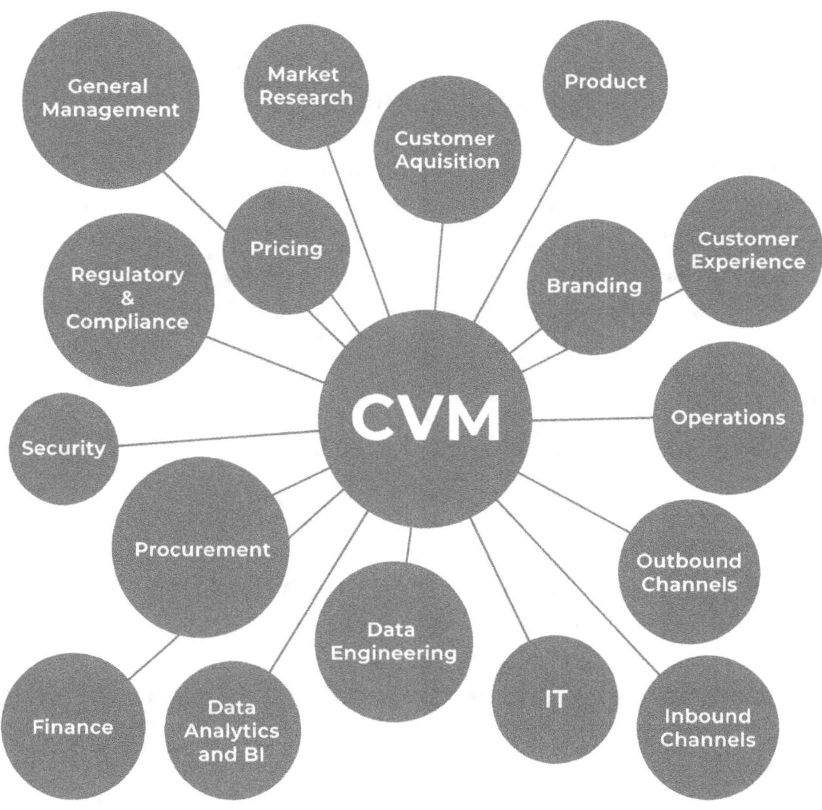

Figure 5.1: Cross-functional Collaboration

Collaboration across functions like sales, marketing, service, and others provides the capability to work with the complete customer journey. This unified approach empowers you to craft personalized interactions and targeted offers wherever and whenever you may wish to embed them; and all teams contribute data in return. For example, sales teams contribute offer and purchase history, marketing teams share campaign and engagement data, and service teams provide insights from customer support—together forming the foundation of informed CVM strategies.

The depth of collaboration varies depending on the CVM initiative. For example, launching a new product requires close coordination with marketing and product development teams to ensure effective positioning and rollout. Meanwhile, a customer service initiative may demand teamwork with operations and support teams to elevate the CX. By tailoring your collaborative efforts to each initiative, you optimize resources and remain agile in responding to market dynamics.

Overcoming Collaboration Challenges

While collaboration is critical, it comes with its share of challenges. Communication breakdowns are common, making clear channels and regular check-ins indispensable. Conflicting priorities between functions can arise, requiring strong leadership to align everyone around shared CVM objectives. Resistance to change is another barrier—breaking down silos and fostering a collaborative culture are key to overcoming it.

Measuring success in a collaborative environment can also be complex. Defining clear metrics and tracking collective progress are essential to attributing outcomes accurately. Managing the flow of information is equally important—too much can overwhelm teams, while too little can hinder decision-making. Ensuring that data is actionable and accessible is vital for maintaining focus and efficiency.

Collaboration: The Cornerstone of Customer Value Management Success

Ultimately, cross-functional collaboration is not just a beneficial practice—it's the cornerstone of CVM success. CVM teams rely on contributions from across the organization, and, in turn, provide critical insights and strategies that drive overall growth.
The following chapters will delve into the nineteen functional areas that work closely with CVM teams, detailing the inputs they provide,

how you should engage with them, and the outputs you'll deliver to support their success.

5.1 General Management

General management (GM) plays a pivotal role in ensuring that all functions, including CVM, work in alignment with the organization's strategic objectives. This alignment enables CVM teams to focus on impactful initiatives that contribute to both short-term goals and long-term business success.

5.1.1 Inputs: How General Management Impacts Customer Value Management

GM provides the strategic direction and sets performance objectives that guide CVM initiatives. By approving CVM strategies and allocating resources for their execution, GM ensures that CVM teams have the necessary tools to deliver results. GM also monitors the progress and outcomes of these initiatives, helping ensure alignment with broader organizational goals.

5.1.2 Customer Value Management's Collaboration with General Management

CVM teams collaborate with GM by designing and executing strategic initiatives that align with the organization's priorities. This includes implementing retention strategies, upsell and cross-sell campaigns, and other initiatives that directly impact KPIs. CVM teams also report on KPIs and share insights into customer behavior, needs, and trends. These insights enable GM to refine strategic goals and adjust resource allocation to meet evolving market demands.

For example, if GM sets a goal to expand imarket share in a specific segment, CVM teams can design targeted campaigns to acquire and retain customers in that segment. This proactive approach ensures that CVM's efforts contribute directly to the organization's objectives.

5.1.3 Outputs: How Customer Value Management Impacts General Management

CVM initiatives significantly influence the organization's overall performance. Metrics such as revenue, customer base growth, and ARPU are critical indicators that inform GM's strategic decision-making. Additionally, insights provided by CVM teams about customer personas, needs, and behaviors enable GM to make data-driven adjustments to its strategies and resource distribution.

5.1.4 Key Handshakes for Effective Collaboration

Collaboration between GM and CVM teams requires clear communication and alignment on the following aspects:

- Strategic organizational direction and priorities
- KPIs related to CVM
- Resource allocation for CVM initiatives
- Regular sharing of customer insights

These interactions ensure that CVM activities remain relevant and contribute to achieving the organization's overarching goals.

5.1.5 The Impact of Collaboration Quality

A lack of alignment between CVM teams and GM can lead to resource misallocation or a focus on the wrong priorities, ultimately jeopardizing the effectiveness of CVM initiatives. Clear communication, shared objectives, and aligned KPIs are critical to maintaining focus and ensuring that CVM teams support GM in achieving strategic success.

"There is a certain level of innovation required for a CVM team to be effective. Acquiring this innovation is very important to the impact that we are delivering. To do so, there is a strategic importance in internal transformation. Of course, they are under pressure, and CVM is part of the answer for the telecoms. It is part of growth transformation, revenue transformation, and it is also a very important client of AI transformation. It is the right time for all of us to be heard and to seek the position that we should have."

— Marek Wiktor Grabowski, B2C Customer Value Management Director at Orange Poland.

5.2 Data Analytics/Business Intelligence

Data analytics/business intelligence (DA/BI) is a vital enabler for CVM, providing the insights and automation required to understand customer behavior and make informed decisions. It ensures the development of high-quality analytical models that validate hypotheses, predict customer actions, and drive the automation of data-driven CVM processes.

5.2.1 Inputs: How Data Analytics Impacts Customer Value Management

DA teams deliver critical inputs that influence CVM's core activities. They determine the effectiveness of initiatives through robust models and analytics, allowing the CVM teams to focus on strategies that produce the best outcomes. Automation facilitated by analytics enhances the CVM teams' productivity by streamlining processes and ensuring consistent quality and stability in automated operations.

The DA function also supports CVM teams by providing essential insights for key processes such as customer segmentation, behavior analysis, churn prediction, and retention strategies. These inputs are indispensable for tailoring campaigns, tracking impacts, and improving overall CVM effectiveness.

5.2.2 Customer Value Management's Collaboration with Data Analytics

CVM teams rely heavily on DA teams to meet their objectives. The CVM teams set the business requirements for analytical tasks and work with the DA teams to execute critical functions, such as:

- Analytics and reporting
- Campaign management
- Personalization and recommendations
- Predicting customer behavior
- Customer insights and impact tracking

CVM teams also initiate analytical projects to address business challenges, ensure that feedback is integrated into refining models, and aligns analytics efforts with organizational goals. This collaboration guarantees that CVM strategies are backed by reliable data and actionable insights.

5.2.3 Outputs: How Customer Value Management Influences Data Analytics

CVM teams determine the scope and direction of analytics activities within their domain. Changes in CVM strategies can lead to updates or overhauls in analytical models, impacting workflows and processes in the analytics team. This interdependency emphasizes the need for ongoing communication to ensure that both teams remain aligned.

5.2.4 The Importance of Effective Collaboration

The collaboration between CVM and DA teams is fundamental to achieving success. Poor alignment between these teams can severely affect CVM's ability to perform effectively, underscoring the need for seamless integration and cooperation.

"We've been in the same place where adding new data or a new machine learning model was a challenge for three to six months. Right now, it's more like several machine learning models, even more than ten, per three-week sprint. It is possible, but it requires a high level of automation and development in MLOps. Cloud technology has been one of the game-changers, giving extra time for data scientists to experiment with new approaches to their models and data. However, the entire value chain must be in place—from machine learning scoring to NBA, campaign systems, and CRM. In many telecoms, these are not fully integrated, creating manual interfaces and making automation difficult."

— Marek Wiktor Grabowski, B2C Customer Value Management Director at Orange Poland

5.3 Data Engineering

Data engineering (DE) teams play a crucial role in enabling CVM by ensuring that customer data is collected, integrated, and readily accessible for decision-making, process automation, and performance measurement. This collaboration directly impacts the effectiveness and efficiency of CVM activities.

5.3.1 Inputs: How Data Engineering Impacts Customer Value Management

DE provides the foundational infrastructure for handling customer data, which is essential for CVM's operations. It ensures the availability of high-quality data, enabling CVM teams to make informed decisions and automate processes efficiently. Reliable data supports analytics, reporting, campaign management, personalization, and customer insights. It also impacts the stability of automated CVM processes and the credibility of reporting.

For example, access to real-time customer usage data allows CVM teams to launch targeted campaigns and track their performance effectively. Accurate data ensures that CVM teams can deliver personalized offers, predict churn, and evaluate the success of initiatives, enhancing the overall productivity of the CVM team.

5.3.2 Customer Value Management's Collaboration with Data Engineering

CVM teams define data requirements and collaborate with the DE teams to ensure that these needs are met. This includes owning projects related to restructuring customer data and providing feedback on data quality and completeness. The DE teams use this input to design systems that support key CVM activities, such as:

- Analytics and reporting
- Personalization and recommendations
- Campaign management
- Customer insights and impact tracking

Changes in CVM strategies often require updates to data pipelines, which necessitates close coordination to minimize disruptions. CVM teams also drive the prioritization of DE projects related to customer, campaign, and value management domains.

5.3.3 Outputs: How Customer Value Management Impacts Data Engineering

CVM teams influence the workload of DE teams by initiating requirements for data pipelines and automation. CVM initiatives often dictate the need for timely and accurate data feeds. Automation of CVM processes adds additional demands, including service-level agreements for data pipeline availability and reliability. Changes in CVM design or implementation may lead to the refactoring of data pipelines, emphasizing the importance of a collaborative approach.

5.3.4 Key Handshakes for Effective Collaboration

To ensure successful collaboration, CVM and DE teams must focus on the following:

- Designing data warehouses and models tailored to CVM's analytical needs
- Implementing efficient ETL processes to streamline data preparation
- Ensuring real-time data feeds for timely decision-making
- Establishing monitoring and testing mechanisms to maintain operational continuity

CVM teams should act as effective internal customers by clearly communicating requirements, prioritizing needs, and providing timelines. Regular alignment meetings and shared KPIs help both teams stay focused on shared objectives.

5.3.5 The Importance of Collaboration Quality

The quality of collaboration between CVM and DE teams directly affects CVM's ability to execute impactful initiatives. Misalignment can lead to disruptions in data availability, inaccuracies in reporting, and inefficiencies in campaign execution. Clear communication, mutual understanding, and proactive alignment are critical to maintaining a productive partnership.

5.4 Customer Acquisition

Customer acquisition (CA) teams are responsible for bringing new customers into the organization through sales and marketing campaigns. This collaboration is critical for ensuring that acquired customers align with CVM goals and contribute to sustainable revenue growth.

5.4.1 Inputs: How Customer Acquisition Impacts Customer Value Management

The CA teams provide a steady stream of new customers, which drives CVM initiatives. Without alignment, however, acquisition efforts can result in challenges such as:

- Attracting fraudulent or fake customers

- Bringing in customers who do not align with the value proposition (e.g., low-price customers who churn quickly)

- Cannibalizing existing customers or products (e.g., offering discounts that prompt existing customers to cancel and resubscribe at lower prices)

- Overpromising value, leading to customer dissatisfaction and complaints

To minimize these risks, CVM teams must ensure that acquisition offers are designed to align with retention and revenue goals.

5.4.2 Customer Value Management's Collaboration with Customer Acquisition

CVM teams work closely with CA teams to mitigate risks and ensure effective onboarding, retention, and upsell strategies. Key areas of collaboration include:

- Designing acquisition offers that avoid cannibalization of existing revenue

- Running the onboarding process for new customers to ensure a seamless transition

- Implementing retention initiatives that keep acquired customers engaged

- Launching upsell and cross-sell campaigns to increase customer value over time

For example, if acquisition campaigns target specific customer segments, CVM teams can use onboarding tools and retention programs tailored to these groups, increasing the likelihood of long-term engagement.

5.4.3 Outputs: How Customer Value Management Impacts Customer Acquisition

CVM teams provide critical insights that inform acquisition strategies. These insights include:

- Onboarding, retention, and revenue KPIs for new customers

- The impact of acquisition campaigns on the existing customer base

- Data on customer demographics, channels, and regions that perform better than average

By sharing this information, CVM teams help the CA teams refine targeting and improve campaign outcomes. For example, CVM teams can identify high-performing acquisition channels or customer segments that generate higher retention rates, enabling CA teams to prioritize these areas.

5.4.4 Key Handshakes for Effective Collaboration

Close alignment between CVM and CA teams is essential for success. Key areas of collaboration include:

- **Pricing strategies:** To balance acquisition efforts with retention goals and prevent cannibalization

- **Segment targeting:** To ensure that acquisition campaigns attract the right customer profiles

- **Shared KPIs:** To align acquisition and retention metrics, such as ARPU and churn rates
- **Data integration:** To combine acquisition and existing customer data for deeper insights
- **Investment tracking:** To analyze marketing ROI and improve future campaign efficiency

Regular communication and shared objectives ensure that both teams are aligned in their efforts.

5.4.5 The Impact of Collaboration Quality

"Poor alignment with the CA team can have severe consequences for CVM. Missteps in pricing or targeting can lead to higher churn, lower ARPU, and reduced customer satisfaction. Strong communication, shared KPIs, and collaboration on strategy design are critical to achieving mutually beneficial outcomes. From the very beginning we have, let's say, an awareness stage. Then we have a stage of conversion. Conversion mostly happens in a certain funnel. Then after conversion, you have onboarding. Onboarding means you have to get the customer into a state where they will start to use the product flawlessly. For example, let's say you convert into a user of Tinder. If you don't upload your photo, provide a decent bio, or list your interests, most likely you won't get matches. If you don't get matches, even if you allow location tracking, your probability to get a match will decrease sharply. In this case, you will fail during activation, which is defined as a certain period dedicated to creating a habit of app usage. A habit can be defined as the customer reaching a certain frequency of product usage during a set time period."

— Mantas Ratomskis, Head of Marketing at Scandagra Lithuania

"By marrying the data with specific indicators or attributes you build ad hoc based on the use case, you might not get the best model in terms of minimum error, but you will get a model that addresses the business needs and is easy to understand by those who use it."

— Silvia Gomez Dominguez, Senior Director, Customer Solutions

5.5 Product Management

Product management (PM) teams ensure that customer needs are met through well-designed product value propositions. Their role directly impacts the success of CVM by shaping the products and features that customers interact with daily.

5.5.1 Inputs: How Product Management Impacts Customer Value Management

PM teams provide the core value proposition and define the CX. CVM teams operate within the boundaries set by product capabilities, which must align with the needs of customer personas. PM teams also deliver critical data for CVM activities, such as purchase history, usage behavior, and technical attributes.

Misaligned product design or deployment, however, can create challenges for CVM teams, such as:

- Introducing products that replace older ones without addressing customer needs, leading to complaints or churn

- Launching uncompetitive features that fail to resonate with the market

- Deploying products with usability issues, impacting customer satisfaction and retention

These inputs significantly influence the CVM teams' ability to execute successful upsell, cross-sell, and retention strategies.

5.5.2 Customer Value Management's Collaboration with Product Management

CVM teams work closely with PM teams to align product features and marketing strategies. This collaboration ensures that:

- New product launches include clear onboarding and customer education processes
- Upsell and cross-sell initiatives are supported by relevant product features
- Customer feedback is incorporated into future product iterations
- Product usage statistics are incorporated into the data warehouse, so that user behavior can be analyzed properly

For example, if the CVM team identifies strong interest in specific product features, this insight can guide the PM team in prioritizing enhancements that meet customer demands.

5.5.3 Outputs: How Customer Value Management Impacts Product Management

CVM teams provide actionable insights to PM teams based on customer behavior and market performance. These insights include:

- Data on product adoption, retention, and revenue metrics
- Feedback on product usability and alignment with customer needs
- Identifying high-performing customer segments, channels, and locations to improve targeting

For example, the CVM team can highlight a particular demographic that adopts a product more frequently, enabling the PM team to refine features or develop tailored bundles.

5.5.4 Key Handshakes for Effective Collaboration

To ensure alignment, CVM and PM teams need to collaborate on the following:

- **Data sharing:** Coordinating on data collection and usage patterns to refine customer segments
- **Feature alignment:** Ensuring that products support the CVM teams' ability to personalize offers and meet customer expectations
- **Joint development:** Collaborating on product bundles and channel strategies to optimize visibility and engagement

These handshakes help both teams stay aligned and deliver products that resonate with customers.

5.5.5 The Impact of Collaboration Quality

A lack of alignment between CVM and PM teams can lead to mismatched customer expectations, poor product adoption, and increased churn. Clear communication, shared objectives, and consistent feedback loops are essential for maintaining a productive partnership.

> *"So it's about the speed, about the quality, and about the price and everything in between. If you are faster, a little bit, if you are better, or if you are cheaper a little bit, then it's more value for the customer. So that's a really broad definition."*

— Ignas Brazdauskas, CEO at Spark Lithuania

> *"Specifically, when it comes to the price point, this is the quickest thing to change, but also the hardest thing to change, right? Because it does contain lots of sensitivity around it."*

— Ignas Brazdauskas, CEO at Spark Lithuania

5.6 Pricing

Pricing teams are responsible for developing a pricing architecture that balances competitiveness and profitability while meeting the needs of both new and existing customers. Effective collaboration between the pricing and CVM teams ensures that pricing strategies align with customer preferences and support business objectives.

5.6.1 Inputs: How Pricing Impacts Customer Value Management

Pricing teams provide the core architecture within which CVM teams operate, setting the parameters for customer segmentation, retention, upselling, and premium offerings. Pricing decisions directly influence revenue and profitability KPIs, and accurate implementation in IT systems ensures smooth execution of CVM campaigns.

Pricing errors or misalignments, however, can cause significant issues, such as:

- Bill shock leading to complaints and churn

- Uncompetitive pricing that drives customers to competitors

- Mismatched pricing levels that disrupt CVM initiatives like discounts for retention or upsell campaigns

The pricing team's role is critical in preventing such issues and enabling the CVM team's ability to execute effective, personalized offers.

5.6.2 Customer Value Management's Collaboration with Pricing

CVM and pricing teams work closely to design strategies that align with customer needs and market dynamics. This collaboration involves:

- Validating CVM offers against the overall pricing architecture

- Providing feedback on the performance of different price points in the customer base

- Collaborating on introducing price increases or temporary reductions

- Ensuring pricing flexibility to support segmentation and tailored campaigns

For example, the CVM team may identify that a particular price point drives retention among high-value customers, prompting adjustments in the pricing strategy to reinforce loyalty.

5.6.3 Outputs: How Customer Value Management Impacts Pricing

CVM teams deliver critical insights that inform pricing decisions. These include:

- Analysis of customer preferences and segment-specific price sensitivity
- Feedback on the performance of price points, including their impact on adoption, retention, and ARPU
- Identification of trends and opportunities, such as bundles or discounts that outperform standard pricing models

For example, if data shows that temporary discounts on data plans increase prepaid customer retention, the pricing team can incorporate similar strategies to optimize revenue.

5.6.4 Key Handshakes for Effective Collaboration

To ensure effective collaboration, CVM and pricing teams must align on:

- **Dynamic pricing tools:** Enabling personalized offers for customer retention and upselling
- **Balancing profitability:** Designing discounts and promotions that maintain financial sustainability
- **Elasticity principles:** Employing pricing strategies based on customer demand and behavior analysis

Regular feedback loops, shared KPIs, and joint planning sessions are crucial for maintaining alignment and responsiveness to market changes.

5.6.5 The Impact of Collaboration Quality

Misalignment between CVM and pricing teams can lead to customer dissatisfaction, increased churn, and missed revenue opportunities. Clear communication, shared goals, and flexibility in pricing design are essential to avoid these issues and ensure mutual success.

> *"Validity, of course, is something that, especially for the prepaid hand, is something that you can change for this particular customer. Because if you know you're traveling for two days only, you might not offer the package that will be seven days valid, and this will only fit that particular customer. So you're basically building a more personalized pricing as well as part of it."*

> — Ignas Brazdauskas, CEO at Spark Lithuania

> *"You will try to close the gaps with your CVM for pricing that might be there. So kind of very interesting combination, super simple, and then really diverse and flexible."*

> — Ignas Brazdauskas, CEO at Spark Lithuania

5.7 Branding

Branding teams play a crucial role in shaping a compelling visual and textual representation of the organization's identity. Their work ensures that CVM campaigns are aligned with the brand's tone, visuals, and messaging, creating a cohesive CX.

5.7.1 Inputs: How Branding Impacts Customer Value Management

Branding decisions directly influence how customers perceive and engage with CVM initiatives. By providing brand guidelines, messaging templates, and marketing assets, the branding teams enable CVM teams to create campaigns that resonate with customers and reinforce the brand identity.

At an operational level, branding teams provide tools such as:

- Visual and tone-of-voice guidance for customer communication

- Ready-to-use marketing assets for major CVM campaigns

- A brand book that sets the standards for consistency across all customer touchpoints

Without alignment, CVM campaigns risk misusing brand assets, leading to disjointed messaging and a diluted CX.

5.7.2 Customer Value Management's Collaboration with Branding

CVM teams integrate branding elements into their campaigns to ensure that communication appeals to the target audience. Collaboration with branding teams involves:

- Preparing inputs and requests for new marketing assets based on upcoming CVM initiatives

- Incorporating brand messaging into customer communications at the right moments of truth

- Aligning communication templates with the brand's visual and textual guidelines

For example, a retention campaign targeting high-value customers might emphasize premium branding elements to convey exclusivity and reliability. This approach reinforces the brand's values while improving campaign performance.

5.7.3 Outputs: How Customer Value Management Impacts Branding

CVM teams provide valuable feedback to the branding teams about how customers respond to brand messaging. Insights include:

- Performance metrics for campaigns using specific branding assets

- Customer preferences that can guide updates to brand narratives

- Trends that can shape future branding strategies, such as a growing interest in sustainability

For example, if data shows that customers value eco-friendly practices, the CVM team can recommend incorporating this theme into the brand narrative to maintain relevance.

5.7.4 Key Handshakes for Effective Collaboration

To ensure success, the CVM and branding teams must align on several key aspects:

- **Customer segmentation:** Tailoring brand messaging for specific customer groups

- **Collaborative campaign creation:** Working together to design and evaluate marketing materials

- **Feedback and refinement:** Adjusting branding elements based on campaign engagement data

- **Risk management:** Reviewing communications to eliminate errors and avoid brand risks

Regular collaboration ensures that all communications are consistent with the brand identity while meeting the unique needs of different customer segments.

5.7.5 The Impact of Collaboration Quality

Misalignment between CVM and branding teams can lead to poor customer engagement and weakened brand trust. Errors in messaging, such as using outdated visuals or unapproved content, can damage the organization's reputation. Strong communication, shared guidelines, and regular feedback are essential to prevent these issues.

"Anything that we do as a CVM function, is it profitable for us or not? It's pivotal to measure right on regular intervals. It's very important for us to measure what is working for us, what is not working for us. This is how I see measurement is the key when it comes to a CVM function."

— Amit Khanna, Marketing Consultant at MTN Ivory Coast

— Amit Khanna, Marketing Consultant at MTN Ivory Coast

5.8 Assisted Inbound Channels

Assisted inbound channel teams are crucial partners for CVM teams, managing customer interactions through physical stores, phone support, and human-assisted chat. These channels are often the first point of contact for customers, making them critical for delivering CVM initiatives effectively.

5.8.1 Inputs: How Assisted Inbound Channels Impact Customer Value Management

Assisted inbound channel teams act as gatekeepers for CVM teams by directly interacting with customers during key moments of truth, such as resolving issues, exploring offers, or providing feedback. Their role impacts CVM in several ways:

- Offering insights into customer needs and preferences, which helps refine CVM strategies

- Serving as the front line for delivering personalized recommendations and upselling opportunities

- Ensuring that customer concerns and feedback are addressed promptly, enhancing satisfaction

Misalignment between CVM and assisted inbound channel teams can hinder CVM's effectiveness. For example, if agents lack access to the latest offers or communication templates, it may result in missed opportunities or customer dissatisfaction.

5.8.2 Customer Value Management's Collaboration with Assisted Inbound Channels

CVM teams support the assisted inbound channel teams by providing tools and training to improve their performance and ensure alignment with CVM objectives. This includes:

- Creating and delivering targeted offers, scripts, and templates that agents use daily

- Training agents on the details of CVM programs, ensuring consistent messaging

- Tracking the teams' performance in executing CVM programs and addressing gaps

- Designing compensation or bonus systems that align with CVM goals, such as incentivizing upselling or retention

For example, if a retention campaign is launched, the CVM team ensures that agents have the necessary information and guidance to promote it effectively, tailoring their interactions to customer profiles.

5.8.3 Outputs: How Customer Value Management Impacts Assisted Inbound Channels

CVM teams significantly influence the performance of the assisted inbound channel teams by:

- Steering the teams toward relevant offers and programs that contribute to achieving revenue and retention KPIs

- Providing insights into customer responses, which help refine scripts and offers

- Reducing operational risks, such as avoiding overloaded queues caused by poorly communicated campaigns or irrelevant offers

Mistakes in CVM messaging, such as errors in campaign texts or misaligned scripts, can lead to overloading the assisted inbound channels team, impacting their ability to handle customer interactions effectively.

5.8.4 Key Handshakes for Effective Collaboration

Alignment between CVM and assisted inbound channel teams is essential for success. Key areas of collaboration include:

- **Offer and message information:** Ensuring that agents have the latest updates on CVM programs to provide accurate information to customers
- **Message conversion tracking:** Helping agents register feedback and conversions for continuous improvement
- **Campaign planning:** Aligning CVM campaign schedules with the channel's capacity plans
- **Team education:** Training the assisted inbound channels team on CVM initiatives and their implementation

Clear communication and regular feedback loops are vital to maintaining alignment and delivering successful campaigns.

5.8.5 The Impact of Collaboration Quality

Strong collaboration with assisted inbound channel teams enables CVM teams to achieve their KPIs by ensuring that agents are equipped to execute initiatives effectively. Poor alignment, however, can result in disjointed messaging, overburdened teams, and missed opportunities to engage customers, ultimately affecting CVM performance.

"There are technically five pillars to build a proper inbound platform. Number one, analytics is key. It's very important to collect all information into one place, analyze customer behavior, and look at different stages of the customer lifecycle before acting."

— Amit Khanna, Marketing Consultant at MTN Ivory Coast

"If you see that, you know, a consumer bought a weekly bundle, and the next day morning, we change the offer, does it have any relevance? It does not. What is important is we need to look at the potential of a consumer and not keep stretching customers every day."

— Amit Khanna, Marketing Consultant at MTN Ivory Coast

5.9 Digital Inbound Channels

Digital inbound channels, such as mobile apps, websites, chatbots, IVRs, and USSD platforms, are critical touchpoints where customers independently engage with the business. These channels serve as a primary interface for exploring services, making purchases, and resolving issues, making their alignment with CVM teams essential.

5.9.1 Inputs: How Digital Inbound Channels Impact Customer Value Management

The digital inbound channels provide real-time insights into customer behavior, preferences, and needs. This data allows CVM teams to refine offers, tailor communication, and optimize customer journeys. However, if these channels fail to integrate with CVM strategies, a significant portion of results becomes unachievable.

For example, when a customer browses a specific service on the mobile app, the channel must capture this intent and present personalized recommendations aligned with the CVM team's objectives. These interactions generate some of the largest customer data streams, which must be properly captured and utilized.

5.9.2 Customer Value Management's Collaboration with Digital Inbound Channels

CVM teams collaborate with digital inbound channels to design and implement seamless CXs. This involves:

- Providing personalized offers based on customer profiles and historical data

- Training and educating digital inbound channel teams on CVM programs to ensure proper execution

- Tracking and analyzing the performance of offers and personalization efforts within these channels

- Contributing to the design of system requirements to support the smooth delivery of CVM programs

For example, CVM teams ensure that promotional banners for loyalty rewards are displayed prominently in the mobile app, targeting the right segments at the right time.

5.9.3 Outputs: How Customer Value Management Impacts Digital Inbound Channels

CVM teams directly influence the performance of digital inbound channels by:

- Steering customer interactions toward relevant products and services to meet revenue and retention KPIs
- Enhancing the usability of these platforms by integrating well-designed, personalized interfaces
- Preventing overburdening the channel with excessive or irrelevant options, which could lead to a poor user experience

Mistakes such as errors in personalization or overwhelming interfaces with too many choices can cause frustration, reduce engagement, and tarnish the CX. Success, on the other hand, can lead to higher traffic volumes that require capacity planning to manage effectively.

5.9.4 Key Handshakes for Effective Collaboration

To ensure alignment, CVM and digital inbound channel teams must collaborate on:

- **Offer and message integration:** Ensuring that platforms can deliver personalized, contextually relevant offers
- **Performance tracking:** Monitoring customer interactions to refine personalization strategies
- **Campaign planning:** Synchronizing campaigns with the channel's capabilities to avoid operational bottlenecks
- **Team training:** Educating digital teams on CVM initiatives to ensure proper execution
- **Feedback loops:** Incorporating customer insights from digital interactions to optimize future campaigns

These handshakes ensure that CVM and digital inbound channel teams work together to create a seamless and impactful CX.

5.9.5 The Impact of Collaboration Quality

Strong collaboration with digital inbound channel teams enables CVM teams to deliver highly personalized, effective campaigns. Poor alignment, however, can lead to missed opportunities, customer dissatisfaction, and diminished engagement. Ensuring consistent communication and shared goals between teams is critical for success.

5.10 Assisted Outbound Channels

Assisted outbound channel teams proactively engage customers through phone calls, in-person appointments, or on-site services. These channels are among the most impactful tools for CVM teams, enabling personalized outreach to drive sales, increase retention, and build loyalty. However, they are also among the most resource-intensive, making efficient collaboration critical for success.

5.10.1 Inputs: How Assisted Outbound Channels Impact Customer Value Management

Assisted outbound channel teams play a significant role in CVM by directly interacting with customers during key moments of truth. These interactions:

- Provide insights into customer preferences and needs, helping CVM teams refine strategies

- Generate qualitative data through recorded conversations, which can serve as a valuable source of market research

- Serve as a feedback loop for assessing the effectiveness of CVM campaigns and offers

For example, through in-person appointments, agents can identify why customers are hesitant to upgrade to premium services, providing actionable feedback for future CVM initiatives.

5.10.2 Customer Value Management's Collaboration with Assisted Outbound Channels

CVM teams collaborate with assisted outbound channel teams to ensure that their efforts align with campaign goals and customer expectations. Key areas of collaboration include:

- Delivering accurate target groups, personalized offers, and clear scripts to support daily interactions
- Providing training on the specifics of CVM campaigns, ensuring that agents understand the objectives and how to communicate them effectively
- Tracking and analyzing the performance of outbound activities to identify areas for improvement
- Designing compensation and bonus systems that incentivize desired outcomes, such as selling high-margin products or retaining high-value customers

For example, if a churn prevention campaign targets at-risk customers, the CVM team equips the assisted outbound channels team with tailored retention offers, increasing the likelihood of customer engagement.

5.10.3 Outputs: How Customer Value Management Impacts Assisted Outbound Channels

CVM teams directly influence the performance of assisted outbound channel teams by:

- Steering customer interactions toward profitable products and services
- Enhancing the CX with relevant, personalized messaging
- Avoiding inefficiencies, such as targeting the wrong customers or overloading agents with unrealistic KPIs

Errors in CVM execution, such as providing outdated offers or inaccurate target groups, can lead to customer dissatisfaction and wasted resources. Success, however, can result in higher engagement, improved conversion rates, and stronger customer relationships.

5.10.4 Key Handshakes for Effective Collaboration

To ensure alignment and efficiency, CVM and assisted outbound channel teams must collaborate on:

- **Accurate targeting:** Delivering correct customer lists and personalized offers to avoid repetitive or irrelevant outreach
- **Feedback loops:** Gathering insights from agent interactions to refine future campaigns and offers
- **Campaign planning:** Aligning campaign schedules with team capacity to prevent overloading during peak periods
- **Training and education:** Ensuring that agents are well-versed in CVM initiatives and equipped to address customer needs effectively
- **Data sharing:** Utilizing shared CRM systems to provide real-time customer information for personalized outreach

These handshakes ensure that assisted outbound channel teams are empowered to deliver high-quality interactions that align with the CVM team's goals.

5.10.5 The Impact of Collaboration Quality

Poor collaboration with assisted outbound channel teams can lead to inefficiencies, such as missed opportunities, resource wastage, and customer frustration. Strong alignment, on the other hand, ensures that agents are equipped to deliver meaningful interactions, driving customer satisfaction and retention.

"We tested a lot. Do we put a general message or a really specific one? Do we say, "Go on Netflix and watch the movies?" Or do we say, "Today this is the best movie for you, like the top movie in Serbia?" More concrete messages, depending on the lifestyle, bring us higher open rates and click rates."

— Irena Radokanović, CRM Automation and Customer Engagement Team Manager at A1 Serbia

5.11 Digital Outbound Channels

Digital outbound channels, including email, SMS, app push notifications, and social media, are vital tools for CVM, enabling broad, cost-effective, and highly personalized customer outreach. These channels allow CVM to engage thousands or even millions of customers at scale, making alignment essential for success.

5.11.1 Inputs: How Digital Outbound Channels Impact Customer Value Management

Digital outbound channels offer several advantages for CVM by:

- Enabling direct, large-scale interaction with customers through personalized communication

- Providing insights from click logs and customer engagement metrics, which inform campaign effectiveness

- Facilitating outreach that influences customer perceptions and drives buying decisions

The effectiveness of these channels, however, depends on their development and integration. If channels are overutilized or poorly aligned with CVM initiatives, they risk delivering irrelevant messages or becoming a source of customer frustration.

5.11.2 Customer Value Management's Collaboration with Digital Outbound Channels

CVM works closely with outbound channels to ensure that campaigns are effective, targeted, and relevant. Key aspects of collaboration include:

- Designing campaigns with accurate target groups and personalized offers

- Ensuring that communication aligns with CX, linking campaigns to actionable goals such as upgrades or renewals

- Tracking the performance of campaigns to refine strategies over time

- Providing clear templates, scripts, and assets to ensure consistency in messaging

For example, a campaign targeting customers with expiring contracts might use SMS notifications to offer exclusive renewal discounts, increasing retention while boosting ARPU.

5.11.3 Outputs: How Customer Value Management Impacts Digital Outbound Channels

CVM plays a crucial role in the success of digital outbound channels by:

- Steering customer interactions toward relevant products and services, enhancing KPIs such as revenue and retention

- Preventing inefficiencies such as overlapping or conflicting campaigns, which can lead to customer fatigue

- Delivering high-quality data and offers, ensuring that communications remain engaging and effective

Mistakes in execution, such as sending repetitive messages or misaligned offers, can reduce engagement and risk messages being flagged as spam. Success, however, strengthens the channel's reputation and boosts customer trust.

5.11.4 Key Handshakes for Effective Collaboration

To maintain alignment, CVM and digital outbound channel teams collaborate on several critical areas:

- **Accurate targeting:** Delivering precise customer lists with personalized recommendations ensures relevance and minimizes repetitive contact.

- **Feedback loops:** Tracking conversions and customer responses provides data for continuous campaign improvement.

- **Campaign planning:** Synchronizing campaign schedules with channel capacity prevents server overload and ensures timely delivery.

- **Data collection:** Utilizing detailed engagement metrics, such as click-through rates and open rates, enhances future targeting and segmentation.

- **Technical monitoring:** Ensuring system stability during large campaigns minimizes disruptions and maintains customer trust.

5.11.5 The Impact of Collaboration Quality

Strong collaboration with digital outbound channels enables CVM to deliver timely, personalized, and effective campaigns that drive customer engagement. Poor alignment, on the other hand, risks overloading systems, diluting campaign effectiveness, and frustrating customers with irrelevant or excessive communication.

"SMS is for me slightly more sensitive.... You need to be more careful when you use SMS because you are directly intruding in someone's life that way. It's not like you open an app and see an email. You get a notification, and it lands in your inbox. It's less rich content, so you have to be very exact and specific. But I would say SMS works very well when used wisely."

— Matthew Robert Tilling, Head of CRM at Telia (no longer with the company)

5.12 Market Research

Market research teams provide critical insights into the market, customer personas, and emerging needs. These insights go beyond the data available in customer profiles or data warehouses, enabling CVM to adapt its strategies to align with market dynamics and customer expectations.

5.12.1 Inputs: How Market Research Impacts Customer Value Management

Market research teams deliver essential information that supports CVM in designing effective initiatives. Their inputs include:

- Customer personas and segmentation insights

- Data on customer needs, preferences, and satisfaction

- Feedback on pricing strategies and gaps in offerings

- Analysis of the competitive landscape and differentiation opportunities

- Recommendations for effective communication strategies

These insights empower CVM teams to refine their campaigns, pricing, and segmentation, ensuring that they resonate with the target audience. For example, if the market research team identifies dissatisfaction with current pricing structures, the CVM team can use this data to adjust offers and improve retention.

5.12.2 Customer Value Management's Collaboration with Market Research

CVM teams work with market research teams to integrate their findings into actionable strategies. This collaboration involves:

- Using market insights to create new campaigns or adjust existing ones

- Sharing trends and data from the customer base to enhance market research accuracy

- Formulating specific requests for studies on emerging customer needs or competitor actions

For example, if the CVM team notices a rise in customer interest in data privacy, this can prompt the market research team to explore deeper insights into customer concerns, enabling both teams to address this need strategically.

5.12.3 Outputs: How Customer Value Management Impacts Market Research

CVM teams provide valuable data and trends that shape the focus of market research. These outputs include:

- Insights from customer interactions, such as satisfaction scores or feature adoption rates

- Data on campaign performance, which helps refine hypotheses for future research

- Observations of customer behavior that reveal potential gaps in offerings or emerging trends

This feedback loop ensures that market research teams deliver relevant, actionable insights to support CVM initiatives.

5.12.4 Key Handshakes for Effective Collaboration

To maximize the value of their partnership, CVM and market research teams must:

- **Establish clear communication:** Regular meetings and information-sharing processes help both teams stay aligned.

- **Prioritize data requests:** Focusing on high-impact research ensures efficient use of resources.

- **Integrate insights:** Combining market research findings with CVM data creates a comprehensive view of customer needs and market conditions.

- **Coordinate timelines:** Aligning project timelines ensures that insights are available when needed for key CVM initiatives.

These handshakes enhance the collaboration and prevent duplication of efforts, ensuring that both teams work efficiently toward shared goals.

5.12.5 The Impact of Collaboration Quality

Effective collaboration with market research teams ensures that CVM initiatives are informed by a deep understanding of customer needs and market trends. Poor alignment, however, can lead to duplicated work or delayed insights, reducing the effectiveness of campaigns and strategies.

5.13 Customer Experience

The customer experience (CX) team is responsible for ensuring seamless and consistent customer journeys across all touchpoints, including channels and products. Their work directly impacts how CVM campaigns are perceived and how effectively they drive engagement, satisfaction, and loyalty.

5.13.1 Inputs: How Customer Experience Impacts Customer Value Management

CX teams provide essential inputs that shape the success of CVM initiatives, including:

- Delivering seamless product and channel experiences that enable smooth customer interactions

- Offering feedback on customer complaints to address pain points and refine campaigns

- Measuring CX through metrics like transactional NPS to evaluate the impact of CVM initiatives

For example, when the CX team ensures frictionless navigation for product upgrades, CVM upsell campaigns see higher conversion rates because customers trust the process.

5.13.2 Customer Value Management's Collaboration with Customer Experience

CVM and CX teams work together to ensure that campaigns align with CX and provide a unified experience. Key aspects of collaboration include:

- **Analyzing customer experience data:** Using insights like NPS to measure the quality and effectiveness of CVM campaigns
- **Incorporating customer complaints:** Using complaints as signals to refine targeting and adjust NBA programs
- **Ensuring consistency across channels:** Following CX guidelines to deliver cohesive messaging and avoid conflicting communications

For example, a campaign targeting existing customers with loyalty rewards must align with CX strategies to ensure that offer redemption is easy and friction-free.

5.13.3 Outputs: How Customer Value Management Impacts Customer Experience

CVM initiatives directly influence CX by:

- Creating omnichannel journeys that strengthen trust and build positive relationships with the brand
- Maintaining alignment of pricing and offers across channels to avoid frustration caused by inconsistencies
- Addressing customer feedback by refining offers, improving messaging, or resolving friction points

Misaligned CVM campaigns, however, can create a disjointed experience, leading to dissatisfaction and reduced engagement. Ensuring that campaigns complement the overall customer journey is critical.

5.13.4 Key Handshakes for Effective Collaboration

A solid two-way information exchange between CVM and CX teams is essential. Key collaboration points include:

- **Reducing friction:** Joint initiatives to minimize customer effort and create smooth transitions across touchpoints
- **Aligning communication:** Ensuring consistent messaging across channels, pricing, and offers
- **Avoiding conflicts:** Preventing misalignments that lead to mixed signals or differing treatments across customer segments
- **Feedback loops:** Using CX data to continuously refine and improve CVM initiatives

These handshakes ensure that CVM campaigns enhance, rather than detract from, the overall customer experience.

5.13.5 The Impact of Collaboration Quality

Strong collaboration with CX teams leads to campaigns that not only promote services but also improve customer journeys. Misalignment, however, risks disconnected communications and friction that undermine trust and satisfaction. Consistent coordination and shared KPIs are essential to maintaining alignment and delivering meaningful results.

5.14 Information Technology

Information technology (IT) teams play a critical role in enabling CVM teams by providing the tools and systems needed to execute campaigns effectively. Their work ensures smooth integration, automation, and data accessibility, which are essential for CVM success.

5.14.1 Inputs: How Information Technology Impacts Customer Value Management

IT provides the technological foundation for CVM operations, influencing the efficiency and effectiveness of campaigns. Key contributions include:

- Delivering tools for data collection, analysis, and campaign execution

- Automating repetitive tasks to improve productivity and reduce errors

- Ensuring system integration across CVM and other supporting functions

For example, the IT team might implement a real-time analytics tool that enables the CVM team to track campaign performance and adjust on the fly.

5.14.2 Customer Value Management's Collaboration with Information Technology

CVM teams collaborate with IT teams to identify, deploy, and optimize technology solutions. This collaboration involves:

- Documenting requirements and selecting vendors for new tools

- Assisting with technology rollouts and ensuring user proficiency

- Leveraging technology to support actionable insights and real-time engagement

For example, the CVM team may partner with the IT team to deploy a new customer data platform that enhances segmentation accuracy and campaign personalization.

5.14.3 Outputs: How Customer Value Management Impacts Information Technology

CVM teams drive technological innovation by providing feedback on system performance and highlighting the need for upgrades or replacements. Specific outputs include:

- Recommendations for improving tools to better support CVM goals

- Identifying gaps in automation that can streamline processes and improve efficiency

For example, feedback from the CVM team may lead the IT team to enhance system integration between campaign management tools and CRM platforms.

5.14.4 Key Handshakes for Effective Collaboration

Successful collaboration between CVM and IT teams requires several critical handshakes:

- Technology needs assessment: Working together to create and maintain a technology reference architecture tailored to CVM

- System integration: Ensuring seamless data flow between tools, vendors, and channels to support campaign execution

- Monitoring and maintenance: Regularly reviewing system performance to prevent disruptions and identify areas for improvement

For example, agreeing on API integrations for real-time data sharing enables personalized customer experiences while maintaining system reliability.

5.14.5 The Impact of Collaboration Quality

A lack of alignment with IT teams can severely impact CVM teams' performance, leading to delays, inefficiencies, and missed opportunities. Strong collaboration ensures that technology serves as an enabler rather than a bottleneck for CVM initiatives.

5.15 Security

Security teams play a critical role in CVM by managing operational security risks and ensuring customer data privacy. Their work is essential for maintaining trust and safeguarding sensitive information, which are both crucial for CVM operations.

5.15.1 Inputs: How Security Impacts Customer Value Management

Security teams establish protocols that govern how CVM teams access and handle customer data. These measures:

- Influence the operational efficiency of CVM activities
- Ensure compliance with data privacy regulations
- Impact the usability and integration of CVM technologies

For example, security policies may dictate encryption standards or access controls that affect how CVM teams process customer data for segmentation and targeting.

5.15.2 Customer Value Management's Collaboration with Security

CVM teams work closely with security teams to implement secure practices in all processes. Key collaboration areas include:

- Aligning CVM activities with security policies to ensure compliance
- Securing the handling of customer data to prevent unauthorized access

For example, during the rollout of a new personalization campaign, the CVM team collaborates with the security team to ensure that data flows comply with privacy regulations while maintaining operational efficiency.

5.15.3 Outputs: How Customer Value Management Impacts Security

CVM teams influence security operations by providing feedback on existing measures and highlighting areas for improvement. Specific contributions include:

- Identifying potential risks associated with customer data handling
- Suggesting improvements to security protocols based on operational needs

As CVM teams aggregate highly sensitive customer data into central repositories, this feedback is crucial for ensuring robust security measures.

5.15.4 Key Handshakes for Effective Collaboration

Close collaboration between CVM and security teams is essential to managing risks while supporting operational goals. Key handshakes include:

- **Secure data handling:** Implementing secure procedures for customer segmentation and analysis
- **Access controls:** Ensuring restricted access to CVM tools and platforms
- **Monitoring:** Regularly assessing automated CVM processes to prevent adversarial attacks
- **Audits:** Conducting security audits to evaluate and enhance existing measures

For example, regular reviews of access logs for CVM platforms help detect unauthorized usage and strengthen preventive measures.

5.15.5 The Impact of Collaboration Quality

A lack of alignment with security teams can lead to delays, inefficiencies, or increased risk of data breaches. Effective collaboration ensures that CVM initiatives are secure, compliant, and efficient.

5.16 Regulatory and Compliance

Regulatory and compliance teams ensure that CVM initiatives adhere to applicable laws and regulations. Their role is crucial for maintaining legal compliance while protecting customer data and trust.

5.16.1 Inputs: How Regulatory and Compliance Impacts Customer Value Management

Regulatory requirements shape how CVM teams handle customer data, design communication strategies, and develop product offerings. Key inputs include:

- Guidelines for data collection, handling, and sharing
- Privacy regulations impacting customer communication and profiling
- Rules governing pricing structures and promotion mechanics

For example, data privacy laws like the General Data Protection Regulation (GDPR) dictate how CVM teams can use customer information for targeting and segmentation.

5.16.2 Customer Value Management's Collaboration with Regulatory and Compliance

CVM teams collaborate with regulatory and compliance teams to ensure that all activities meet legal and ethical standards. This includes:

- Aligning data collection and customer communication practices with privacy laws
- Reviewing the use of AI and ML in customer profiling to comply with AI regulations
- Ensuring that pricing and promotion strategies adhere to consumer protection laws
- Responding to internal and external audit requests

For example, before launching a campaign, the CVM team consults with the regulatory and compliance team to confirm that all messaging and offers meet legal requirements.

5.16.3 Outputs: How Customer Value Management Impacts Regulatory and Compliance

CVM teams contribute to regulatory and compliance efforts by:

- Managing customer data within the boundaries of privacy regulations
- Applying AI and predictive models responsibly, ensuring trans-

parency in their use

- Structuring pricing and promotions in alignment with commercial laws

By integrating regulatory and compliance measures into its operations, CVM teams minimize the risk of penalties and enhances customer trust.

5.16.4 Key Handshakes for Effective Collaboration

Collaboration with regulatory and compliance teams focuses on managing risks and ensuring adherence to laws. Key handshakes include:

- **Applying GDPR principles:** Ensuring secure and lawful customer data management

- **Transparent communication:** Crafting compliant customer messaging

- **AI and ML compliance:** Aligning customer profiling practices with regulations

- **Product and pricing strategies:** Structuring offers in accordance with consumer protection laws

- **Monitoring tools:** Leveraging technology for ongoing regulatory and compliance assurance

For example, using automated systems to monitor campaign activities can ensure consistent adherence to legal guidelines.

5.16.5 The Impact of Collaboration Quality

Poor alignment with regulatory and compliance teams can delay CVM initiatives, introduce legal risks, and harm customer trust. Strong collaboration ensures that campaigns are legally compliant and operate smoothly.

5.17 Procurement

Procurement teams are essential for managing vendor contracts, ensuring compliance with legal standards, and securing favorable terms. Their work directly supports CVM teams by enabling access to the tools and services needed for campaign execution and customer engagement.

5.17.1 Inputs: How Procurement Impacts Customer Value Management

Procurement processes and legal reviews significantly influence how quickly and effectively CVM teams can acquire new tools and services. Key inputs include:

- Guidance on contract negotiations and vendor agreements

- Assurance of compliance with legal and regulatory requirements

- Timely resolution of legal reviews to prevent delays in implementing technologies

For example, legal standards for data security may impact the choice of a vendor offering analytics tools, ensuring both compliance and operational efficiency.

5.17.2 Customer Value Management's Collaboration with Procurement

CVM teams collaborate with procurement teams to:

- Identify and select vendors that meet both technical and legal requirements

- Provide detailed use cases and requirements for vendor evaluations

- Ensure that all acquired technologies comply with legal and regulatory standards

- Participate in contract negotiations to secure favorable terms and protect CVM interests

For example, when onboarding a new customer relationship management (CRM) tool, CVM teams work with procurement teams to ensure that the tool's capabilities align with campaign needs while adhering to privacy laws.

5.17.3 Outputs: How Customer Value Management Impacts Procurement

CVM teams provide critical feedback and input that shapes procurement decisions, such as:

- Technical and operational requirements for selecting vendors and tools
- Performance feedback on existing vendors to inform future agreements or adjustments
- Insights on contract compliance to ensure ongoing alignment with CVM goals

For example, the CVM team might highlight inefficiencies with a current vendor, prompting the procurement team to renegotiate terms or explore alternatives.

5.17.4 Key Handshakes for Effective Collaboration

Effective collaboration between CVM and procurement teams relies on:

- **Regular communication:** Scheduled meetings to discuss upcoming needs and projects
- **Clear requirements:** Providing detailed CVM priorities and evaluation criteria for vendor selection
- **Joint contract reviews:** Ensuring that contracts meet both operational and legal standards
- **Ongoing feedback:** Sharing insights on vendor performance for continuous improvement

For example, involving procurement teams early in the planning phase of a new technology acquisition ensures smoother negotiations and faster implementation.

5.17.5 The Impact of Collaboration Quality

Strong alignment with procurement teams ensures that CVM teams can efficiently acquire the necessary tools and services while mitigating legal and operational risks. Poor collaboration, however, can lead to delays, increased costs, and potential compliance issues.

5.18 Finance

Finance teams play a critical role in ensuring that CVM initiatives are adequately funded and aligned with the organization's financial goals. Their oversight helps balance resource allocation between growth strategies and financial stability, enabling CVM teams to deliver impactful customer programs.

5.18.1 Inputs: How Finance Impacts Customer Value Management

Finance teams' decisions determine the scope and scale of CVM campaigns, tools, and technologies. Their inputs include:

- Allocating resources for CVM initiatives based on financial priorities
- Reviewing ROI projections to justify funding requests
- Providing insights into financial performance to guide campaign adjustments

For example, budget allocations might enable CVM to deploy advanced analytics tools for personalized offers, enhancing customer engagement and retention.

5.18.2 Customer Value Management's Collaboration with Finance

CVM teams work with finance teams to:

- Plan and secure funding for campaigns and tools
- Provide financial projections and ROI analyses for proposed initiatives

- Ensure that expenditures align with approved budgets and financial plans
- Report on the financial outcomes of campaigns and initiatives

For example, the CVM team might present a business case for a loyalty program aimed at high-value customers, supported by projected revenue increases and retention improvements.

5.18.3 Outputs: How Customer Value Management Impacts Finance

CVM teams contribute to the organization's financial strategy by:

- Driving revenue through effective campaigns, such as upselling or cross-selling initiatives
- Providing data and insights on campaign performance to inform financial decisions
- Demonstrating ROI to justify continued or increased investment in CVM programs

For example, detailed reports on the ROI of a retention program help prioritize future investments and reinforce the value of CVM initiatives.

5.18.4 Key Handshakes for Effective Collaboration

Effective collaboration between CVM and finance teams relies on several key practices:

- **Regular planning meetings:** Joint sessions to align financial goals and allocate resources effectively
- **Transparent communication:** Clearly articulating the financial implications of CVM projects to secure funding
- **Monitoring and reporting:** Providing real-time updates on campaign performance to enable proactive budget adjustments
- **Financial KPIs:** Developing shared metrics, such as cost-per-acquisition or incremental revenue, to evaluate success and guide investments

For example, during annual planning, the CVM team and the budgeting team might prioritize funding for high-ARPU customer campaigns, ensuring that resources are allocated to maximize impact.

5.18.5 The Impact of Collaboration Quality

Strong collaboration ensures that CVM projects are funded, cost-effective, and aligned with organizational objectives. Poor alignment can lead to delays, funding shortages, and missed opportunities. For example, if additional funding isn't approved promptly for a high-performing campaign, CVM teams may miss critical opportunities to scale their efforts.

5.19 Operations

CVM operations teams are essential for ensuring the smooth execution of CVM initiatives by optimizing workflows, managing resources, and streamlining daily activities. Their involvement allows CVM teams to execute campaigns efficiently while maintaining alignment with organizational priorities.

5.19.1 Inputs: How Operations Impacts Customer Value Management

Operations teams directly affect CVM teams' ability to execute campaigns and initiatives without delays by:

- Streamlining processes for timely data management and analysis
- Coordinating tools and system integration during procurement and implementation
- Ensuring alignment with operational requirements and infrastructure

For example, involving the operations team in the tools acquisition process ensures that new technologies meet organizational and operational needs, avoiding delays in implementation.

5.19.2 Customer Value Management's Collaboration with Operations

CVM teams work with operations teams to:

- Optimize resource allocation and workflows for campaign execution
- Integrate operational data into CVM analytics for better customer insights and targeting
- Align CVM activities with broader organizational strategies and schedules
- Address operational requirements such as API integration, system interoperability, and lifecycle management for new tools

For example, CVM teams collaborate with operations teams to ensure that customer insights flow seamlessly between systems, enabling better campaign personalization.

5.19.3 Outputs: How Customer Value Management Impacts Operations

CVM teams provide valuable data and feedback that operations teams use to:

- Optimize workflows and improve service efficiency
- Identify and resolve operational bottlenecks impacting campaign performance
- Assess the usability and impact of new tools and processes

For example, feedback from a CVM campaign targeting premium customers might reveal inefficiencies in data flow, prompting the operations team to implement system improvements.

5.19.4 Key Handshakes for Effective Collaboration

To ensure effective collaboration, CVM and operations teams should focus on:

- **Regular coordination meetings:** Aligning on timelines, priorities, and resource needs

- **Shared KPIs:** Ensuring that both teams work toward common performance goals

- **Collaborative problem-solving:** Addressing operational challenges together to prevent disruptions

- **Data integration:** Ensuring seamless integration of CVM data with operational systems for process optimization

For example, regular updates on campaign timelines help operations teams allocate resources effectively, avoiding delays and disruptions.

5.19.5 The Impact of Collaboration Quality

Effective collaboration ensures that CVM activities are executed smoothly, with minimal disruptions. Poor alignment can lead to delays, inefficiencies, and unmet requirements, hindering campaign performance. For example, a lack of coordination during a tools acquisition process may result in operational issues that disrupt campaign delivery.

> *"The first check is how your tool will integrate in your complex environment infrastructure. Do you have any API? Do you have any interoperability, flexibility? How will you manage the lifecycle of your tool? What does your tool need to operate or to run in the proper way? What happens if there is an issue with your tool regarding the processes? What are the responsibilities of who you must count on, and what internally in the company do you need to know or need to master? Trainings, information, documentation, architecture, and so on."*

> — Alexis Koalla, Director Operations Strategy and Transformation at Orange

> *"The most common mistake is not considering the operational constraint from the think and build side. Bid could be — make or buy. Internally, I need to master this new tool. What are the skills, the security issues? And what do I need to know about these tools? That will help me when there is an incident or a crisis or a problem, to be able to alert the technical guys—level one, level two, or level three, depending*

on the level of support. So, I will say that the most common mistake is with the documentation sharing with the ops guys. Because you deploy the tool even if it is in CI, CD. The tool could be deployed successfully. But where is the documentation for the ops to be able to be autonomize and master these tools on their own? Documentation is the entry point."

— Alexis Koalla, Director Operations Strategy and Transformation at Orange

6. Conclusions and Next Steps

6.1 Key Takeaways

Customer value management in mature telecom markets is a key shareholder value creation tool. At the same time, it is bewilderingly complex and hard to systematize.

CVM is a multi-faceted, cross-functional organizational capability that requires high levels of experience and seniority, right talent, appropriate organizational designs, a well-crafted product portfolio, the right technology and data architectures, adequate historical data volumes, deep customer behavior insight and mindful strategic execution. None of these are easy, cheap or quick to achieve, suggesting that CVM has all the hallmarks of a durable competitive advantage (or disadvantage).

Given its strategic importance, it is surprising to see that CVM in telecoms has so far eluded comprehensive analysis and systematization efforts, as evidenced by the lack of any meaningful publications. It has been and remains a rare, mystified province of management consultants, scattered ideas, overselling and underdelivery, as well as amazing superstar performers who have, mainly, independently discovered and re-discovered the secret sauce in multiple telecoms across the globe.

Our global surveys and interviews reveal that there are clear organizational patterns, technological approaches, strategic ideas, and typical CVM programs that work again and again. It is a disservice to the industry to keep this know-how locked up for the sake of competitive advantage and not pass it on to the next generation.

This book is our humble attempt to address this oversight, and provides a first systematic treatment of the subject. As a first publication in the field, it is inevitably going to be criticized as missing some crucial elements. We are deeply aware of quite a few important aspects that did not make it into the current edition; however, in the spirit of not letting perfect be the enemy of good, we have decided to move ahead and publish this edition. Our conversations with practitioners in the field suggest that there is loads of value to be obtained already—use it.

We invite you to share your experiences, reactions, insights and suggestions to be incorporated into the next edition for the benefit of the entire customer value management profession in telecoms.

6.2 Engage With Authors And Contributors

Contributors to the *Customer Value Management Body of Knowledge (CVMBoK)* represent a diverse and dedicated group of professionals committed to advancing your understanding and practice of CVM. Their insights and expertise have been instrumental in shaping this resource. CVMBoK authors invite you to become part of this growing contributors list and share your knowledge with the dynamic CVM field.

6.2.1 Authors of the CVMBoK

- Šarūnas Chomentauskas, CEO & Co-founder of Exacaster
- Egidijus Pilypas, Director of Product and Marketing, Co-founder of Exacaster
- Silvia Gomez Dominguez, Senior Director, Customer Solutions
- Kristine Raumane, Head of Customer Value Management at Tele2 Latvia
- Rokas Narkus, Head of Consulting at Exacaster

6.2.2 Contributors to the CVMBoK

CVMBoK was generously contributed to by *CVM Stories* speakers and other industry experts:

- Simon Sanga, Customer Value Manager at M-Pesa
- Matthew Robert Tilling, Head of CRM at Telia (no longer with the company)
- Vytautas Jurkus, Senior Manager for CRM, User Experience and Marketing Automation at Western Union (no longer with the company)
- Ignas Brazdauskas, CEO at Spark Lithuania

- Paulius Grygalis, Manager of Client Intelligence and Client Service at Tele2 Lithuania

- Vaidotas Juknys, Head of Commerce at Smartproxy

- Florian Schwarz, Program Lead in Data-Driven Marketing at A1 Austria

- Ignas Žurauskas, Commercial Director at Exacaster

- Eglė Baradinskienė, Operational Director at Exacaster

- Justas Jankūnas, AI/ML Area Lead at Exacaster

- Thando Mngomezulu, Customer Intelligence Senior Specialist at Vodafone Business

- Sultan Basit Hassan, former Data Center Engineer at Rack Center

- Avinash Sharma, Sr. CRM Manager at OSN

- Shrivatsan Balagopal, AGM Product Management at Vodafone Idea Limited

- Mantas Ratomskis, Head of Marketing at Scandagra Lithuania

- Kaur Elviste, Head of Non-Aeronautical Commercial Services at Tallinn Airport

- Tommy Wahyudi, VP - Head of CVM Data Growth Strategy at Indosat Ooredoo

- Marek Wiktor Grabowski, B2C Customer Value Management Director at Orange Poland

- Sanna Emtinger, Head of CVM & MarTech at Telia Norway

- Elchin Gulmammadov, Group Marketing Director at Azerconnect Group

- Kamaldin Pirimbaev, Manager of Capabilities Unit, Big Data and CVM Department at Kcell AO

- Alberto Arimana Celis, Head of B2B CVM at Entel Peru

- Thierry Awetimbi, CVM Manager at Vodacom Congo (no longer with the company)

- Amit Khanna, Marketing Consultant at MTN Ivory Coast

- Kwame van Eijndhoven, Owner of Kwadata

- Irena Radokanović, CRM Automation and Customer Engagement Team Manager at A1 Serbia
- Alexis Koalla, Director Operations Strategy and Transformation at Orange
- **And this may be you!**

6.3 Enhance the *CVMBoK*: Share Your Insights

6.3.1 Why Contribute?

We believe in the power of collective knowledge. Join the community of CVM professionals, participate in discussions, and collaborate on finding solutions to industry challenges. Share your knowledge and contribute to our growth.

First Access

Be among the first
to access the updated
editions.

Spotlight Opportunity

Chance
to be featured on
CVM Stories Podcast.

Champion Status

Gain recognition as a key
contributor in shaping
the CVM discipline.

Professional Boost

Elevate your professional profile,
especially if you're seeking new
career opportunities!

6.3.2 How to Contribute

Step 1: Review the current *CVMBoK* — Familiarize yourself with the content to see where your expertise can augment our existing knowledge.

Step 2: Submit a proposal — Send us a summary of your contribution idea through an email: **cvmbok@exacaster.com**.

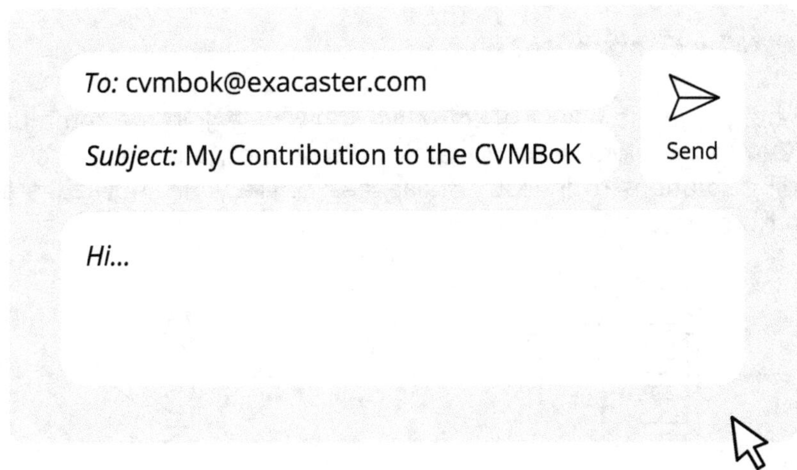

Step 3: Collaboration — If your proposal aligns with our needs, our editorial team will work with you to align and refine your content via a thirty-minute online call.

Step 4: Publication — Once approved, your contributions will be incorporated into the next edition of the *CVMBoK*.

6.4 Complimentary Customer Value Management Resources

The CVMBoK is our cornerstone of knowledge-sharing, but we go further, empowering you to turn knowledge into action and guiding you every step of the way.
Our free CVM resources help you sharpen your CVM strategy, stay informed, and continuously learn from the best.

1. Benchmark Your CVM Performance Against Global Telecoms

Discover how you measure up with the CVM Benchmark—the only telecom-specific assessment that compares your CVM performance to telecom teams worldwide.

http://cvmbenchmark.com

2. One-Hour Consultation with a CVM Expert *

Take it a step further with a CVM Benchmark Consultation—a complimentary video session with a CVM expert to review your assessment and provide actionable guidance.

* You must complete the CVM Benchmark before booking a call.

3. Learn from Industry Leaders and Professionals on the CVM Stories Podcast

Tune in to the CVM Stories podcast, where seasoned professionals share best practices, lessons learned, and strategies that deliver real impact.

http://cvm-stories.com

4. Explore the Future of the Industry with CVM Trends Research

Dive into CVM Trends: Telecom Edition—the first research study on key strategies, tools, and trends shaping the global CVM landscape.

http://cvmtrends.com

6.5 Foundational Literature and Recommended Readings

The documents listed below influenced and shaped many foundational concepts supporting the CVMBoK. Moreover, this curated list includes sources, books, articles, and references that can enhance your understanding of CVM and lead you to more in-depth research or reading on related topics.

6.5.1 Notes

Ribeiro, Hugo et al. 2023. *"Determinants of churn in telecommunication services: A systematic literature review." Management Review Quarterly, Vol. 74,* pp. 1327–64.

6.5.2 Marketing and Customer Value Management

Kotler, P., and Keller, K. L. 2021. *Marketing Management, Global 16th Edition*. Pearson.

McCorkell, G. 1997. *Direct and Database Marketing*. Kogan Page.

Humby, C., Hunt, T., and Phillips, T. 2008. Scoring Points: *How Tesco Continues to Win Customer Loyalty*. Kogan Page.

Manning, H., Bodine, K., and Bernoff, J. 2012. *Outside In: The Power of Putting Customers at the Center of Your Business*. Forrester Research.

Underhill, P. 2008. *Why We Buy: The Science of Shopping—Updated and Revised for the Internet, the Global Consumer, and Beyond*. Simon & Schuster.

Rackham, N. 1989. *Major Account Sales Strategy*. McGraw-Hill.

Phillips, R. 2005. *Pricing and Revenue Optimization*. Stanford Business Books.

Carlzon, J. 1987. *Moments of Truth.* HarperCollins Publishers.

6.5.3 Financial Management and Performance

PKF International Ltd. 2023. *Wiley 2023 Interpretation and Application of IFRS Standards* (Wiley Regulatory Reporting). Wiley.

Kaplan, R. S., and Norton, D. P. 1996. *The Balanced Scorecard: Translating Strategy into Action*. Harvard Business Review Press.

6.5.4 Product Management

Ulwick, A. W. 2016. *Jobs to be Done: Theory to Practice*. IDEA BITE PRESS.

Christensen, C. M., Dillon, K., Hall, T., & Duncan, D. S. (2016). *Competing against luck: The story of innovation and customer choice*. HarperBusiness.

6.5.5 Strategy and Innovation

Rumelt, R. P. 2011. *Good Strategy Bad Strategy*. Crown Business.

Kim, W. C., and Mauborgne, R. A. 2015. *Blue Ocean Strategy*. Harvard Business Publishing Corporation.

Dalio, R. 2017. *Principles: Life and Work*. Simon & Schuster.

6.5.6 Technology and Future Trends

Ford, M. 2018. *Architects of Intelligence: The Truth about AI from the People Building It*. Packt Publishing.

Taylor, J. 2005. *Space Race: An Inside View of the Future of Communications Planning*. John Wiley & Sons.

Rosling, H., Rönnlund, A. R., and Rosling, O. 2018. *Factfulness: Ten Reasons We're Wrong about the World—and Why Things are Better than You Think.* Flatiron Books.

Heffernan, M. 2020. *Uncharted: How to Map the Future Together.* Simon & Schuster.

6.5.7 Personal Development

Sullivan, D., and Hardy, B. 2021. *The Gap and the Gain: The High Achievers' Guide to Happiness*, Confidence, and Success. Hay House Business.

Watanabe, K. 2009. *Problem Solving 101: A Simple Book for Smart People*. Portfolio.

Yankov, S., and Alonso, C. 2021. *PERFORM: The Unsexy Truth about (Startup) Success*. Self-published.

About the Co-Authors

Egidijus Pilypas

Co-founder, Exacaster
and Co-host, CVM Stories

While studying machine learning, Egidijus was invited to join a telecom company as a product marketing manager—now known as customer value management. Egidijus's passion for data and AI, fused with personalized marketing, plunged him into the world of CVM, where his interests and the role harmoniously converged. Together with Šarūnas, Egidijus spotted immense opportunities for telecoms to grow through enhanced CVM, leading them to establish Exacaster—a company focused on accelerating returns on customer value management.

For the past 18 years, Egidijus has been dedicated to discovering CVM best practices, engaging with leading CVM professionals globally. He realized that despite its complexity and significance, CVM work remains unstructured and often unrecognized. Driven to change this, he embarked on a mission to make the CVM field famous. As part of this mission, the co-authors created the CVMBoK—a foundational resource to empower success in the CVM field.

Šarūnas Chomentauskas

CEO and Co-founder, Exacaster

"Customer value management for me is a lifelong passion. By sharing our collective knowledge and using data driven insights we can reliably transform how companies engage with their customers and achieve sustainable growth."

Šarūnas is the CEO and Co-founder of Exacaster, whose mission is to accelerate returns on data, AI, and customer value management with seamless all-in-one services that integrate consulting, products, solutions, and managed services. Before founding Exacaster, Šarūnas built and sold B2C ventures in social networking, e-commerce, online gaming as well as several B2B companies in SaaS and professional services. In addition to his lifelong entrepreneurial career, Šarūnas led the product development and management function at Bitė Group, a leading telecommunications provider in the Baltics. The challenges and experience of wrangling large data sets to obtain customer insight at Bitė laid the foundations for what Exacaster is today. With a lifelong experience of both entrepreneurship and corporate career Šarūnas has established a strong reputation in the tech and telecommunication sectors.

Šarūnas holds a BA in International Business, a BA in Political Science & International Relations, and is a certified information systems auditor. He is an expert in strategic customer value management that focuses on a holistic approach to CVM that includes products, people, organization, data, and technology. He has a proven track record of transforming organizations through implementing strategic, data-driven solutions. Under his guidance, Exacaster landed in Deloitte's Technology Fast 50 Central Europe list multiple times, which recognized it as one of the fastest-growing technology companies in the region. His strategic vision has made Exacaster a trusted partner for telecoms and beyond.

Šarūnas is a frequent speaker on the topic of data-driven business, AI, and entrepreneurship and he is the co-host of the CVM Stories podcast.

Silvia Gomez Dominguez

Senior Director, Customer Solutions

"My career is driven by a passion for transforming businesses through customer obsession and AI-driven innovation. By blending the quantitative and qualitative aspects, I create 'whole of CVM experiences' that connect businesses with their customers in meaningful, measurable, and impactful ways. Building an emotional connection with the customer is my secret super CVM power."

With a unique value proposition at the intersection of customer, marketing, digital, and AI, Silvia Gomez Dominguez is a senior executive celebrated for her authenticity, courage, and ability to build trust. Over her 20-year international career, Silvia has driven customer-centric transformations, AI and digital innovation, and revenue growth strategies across telecommunications, financial services, and consulting industries.

Silvia's career is marked by her expertise in navigating complexity, inspiring high-performing teams, and delivering measurable customer and business outcomes:
As a member of the Centre of Excellence for Revenue Growth, Silvia helped global financial services and telecommunications clients unlock new value. She led customer-centric transformations, embedding AI, digital marketing, and analytics-driven strategies for top-tier clients, balancing customer satisfaction with business goals.

In Australia, Silvia led cross-functional teams, transforming customer value management and customer lifecycle engagement. She implemented cutting-edge MarTech ecosystems, resulting in significant improvements in customer lifetime value, revenue, and EBITDA.
Silvia's work is rooted in a holistic understanding of customer and market dynamics, combining technical expertise with strategic vision:

- Customer Value Management: Designed and executed signature customer journeys, leveraging data-driven insights to build loyalty and revenue.

- Digital Transformation and Innovation: Delivered enterprise-wide digital strategies that integrate AI, MarTech, and data analytics to drive customer-centric growth.

- Revenue Growth and Efficiency: Embedded test-and-learn cultures and operational models, delivering sustainable growth and efficiency across complex environments.

Silvia holds a master's and bachelor's degree in telecommunications engineering from Spain's Polytechnic University of Madrid and an International MBA from Universitat Ramon Llull and Manhattan College in New York. She has also completed advanced programs in big data, digital marketing, and talent management.

Kristine Raumane

Head of the Customer Value Department, Tele2 Latvia

"I believe that a passion for sales can lead to great results in every area of life."

Kristine Raumane harnesses analytical thinking and a results-driven mindset to drive success. With a degree in business psychology, certification as a professional coach, and specialized training in Lean methodologies, Kristine excels in optimizing sales processes and achieving tangible outcomes.

Kristine's journey is marked by a strong enthusiasm for merging business needs with IT development and a keen interest in AI implementation. She specializes in data analysis, both from a big-picture perspective and in the details, ensuring that strategies are both comprehensive and precise. By creating successful integrations and developing effective sales funnels, Kristine consistently delivers measurable results in key areas such as retention, churn reduction, ASPU, and revenue growth.

Kristine is passionate about sharing knowledge through her writing and speaking engagements, aiming to inspire others to embrace analytical approaches and innovative technologies to achieve their goals. Through her work, Kristine strives to cultivate environments where dedication and strategic thinking lead to success in all facets of life.

Rokas Narkus

Head of Consulting, Exacaster

Rokas believes that the value of a customer value manager is the value of the client. By identifying key value drivers and understanding the client's unique context, he strives to create win-win scenarios.

For over a decade, Rokas has worked at the intersection of data, AI, and strategy, helping organizations translate business objectives into actionable solutions. Currently, he leads the consulting area at Exacaster, managing clients across geographies such as Medellín, Colombia, and London, UK, with projects spanning consulting, data engineering, customer profiling, and machine learning implementations. Previously, as a senior consultant at EY, he designed data strategies for leading Baltic enterprises and shaped the economic development strategy for his hometown.

A lifelong learner, Rokas holds MSc and CEMS degrees in Economics and International Management from the Stockholm School of Economics and pursues certifications to stay at the forefront of data and AI.

About the Publisher

"We are here to make your CVM transformation vision work and deliver real business results."

Exacaster was founded by a group of seasoned marketing and data science practitioners on December 3, 2010, and has become one of the fastest-growing companies in Central Europe.

This company helps organizations improve their customer value management processes and achieve superior growth by making more decisions data-driven and focused on delivering great customer experiences.

Exacaster drives results by tackling the biggest CVM transformation challenges—endless delivery cycles, hidden costs, locked systems, lack of guidance, and lack of impact—right from the start. Their comprehensive portfolio spans consulting, future-proof technology solutions, and managed services.

With over 14 years of experience, the company started working with large language models before it was fashionable. They've helped leading telecoms globally—such as Ultra Mobile, Tigo, Mint Mobile, and A1 Austria—meet their customer data needs and drive growth with AI/ML solutions for churn prediction, retention, and personalization.

Since 2010, the company has delivered 100+ projects across eight industries—telecom, finance, insurance, government, logistics, retail, utilities, and pharma.

Deloitte named Exacaster among the top 50 technology companies in the region in 2019. It was selected as one of 1000 Europe's fastest-growing companies by *Financial Times* and Statista in 2020.

Most importantly, Exacaster is on a mission to make CVM widely famous. Through knowledge-sharing initiatives like *CVM Stories*, CVM Certification, and the *Customer Value Management Body of Knowledge (CVMBoK)*, the company is setting a new standard for proven CVM expertise and real impact.

For more information visit exacaster.com.

www.ingramcontent.com/pod-product-compliance
Lightning Source LLC
LaVergne TN
LVHW011005200726
843509LV00011B/993